The handmade loaf

DAN LEPARD

MITCHELL BEAZLEY

THE
handmade
LOAF

DAN LEPARD

To my partner David and my parents
Nancy and Ray

The handmade loaf
by Dan Lepard

First published in Great Britain in 2004 by
Mitchell Beazley, an imprint of Octopus Publishing Group Limited, 2–4
Heron Quays, London E14 4JP.

Octopus Publishing Group Limited 2004
Text & photography © Dan Lepard 2004

ISBN 1 84000 966 7
A CIP catalogue record for this book is available from the British Library.

While all reasonable care has been taken during the preparation of this edition, neither the
publisher, editors, nor the authors can accept responsibility for any consequences arising
from the use thereof or from the information contained therein.

Commissioning Editor: Rebecca Spry
Executive Art Editor: Yasia Williams-Leedham
Design: Lawrence Morton
Photography: Dan Lepard
Editor: Hattie Ellis
Production: Sarah Rogers
Index: John Noble

Typeset in Caslon and Din
Printed and bound by Lego s.p.a.,
Italy

Contents

Introduction

THE HANDMADE LOAF is about making the most of what we have; about appreciating what grows in the soil, what is local, and being economical and resourceful with it. We have so much, too much, that we can buy, yet the basic labour of doing, the making with our own hands, is what enlivens us and makes us feel human. Someone once asked me why I bother mixing and shaping bread by hand. I didn't have the words to answer them, nor could I understand why they didn't just know. I will not let my fingers be reduced to simply button-pressing, dial-twirling or switch-flicking. There is no instrument in my bag of baker's tools more useful and adaptable than my two hands, and as long as I can use them to make and shape bread, I will.

While travelling through northern Europe, I have met people who bake bread in a considered way: bakers who adapt their ingredients according to what is plentiful or scarce at different times of the year. Some bake with wood-fired ovens, some with gas or electric. Some let machines assist them, some bake free-hand. Solitary bakers, and groups of bakers. Many of the recipes that I've written for this book reflect the techniques they use, as well as each baker's response to the ingredients he has at his disposal.

I haven't raided these bakers' personal recipe books, for if I did I couldn't give each community the space it deserves, and nor could I speak their languages well enough to be sure my translations were accurate. But by watching, living, and baking with them, I have distilled the breads we baked into new recipes which walk in the footsteps of those bakers and bring us closer to their traditions. This is the most honest way in which I can convey the breads and methods I encountered, with recipes bakers in other communities can use.

Two steps, though, are significantly different and somewhat heretical. There are no recipes in this book in which the dough is kneaded for 10 minutes on a floured surface, and all the recipes begin with an initial resting period after the ingredients are first combined. After this rest, the dough is kneaded lightly on an oiled surface to combine the ingredients and get the mass even. All the oil does is allow the timid baker to handle sticky dough in a comfortable way, and inhibit the baker from throwing in handfuls of flour in a panic. In time, a scraper and the merest dusting of flour will allow you to achieve the same result. These stages – combined with a gentle manipulation of the dough during an extended rise, giving the yeast time to ferment and aerate – make the soft, sticky dough malleable and easy to shape. All ingredients are weighed, even the water, as this is easy to do with a good set of scales and helps me to translate the handfuls I encountered into something accurate.

The photographs that illustrate the recipes show the actual loaves I baked, made using the instructions given. Most, but not all, were baked (and photographed) in my home, in a gas-fired domestic oven. The temperature dipped up and down during the day, as my neighbours heated their houses or cooked their meals. The thermometer that I hung inside the oven became essential, and told me at what time of the day I was likely to get the oven hot enough, and I'd schedule the baking around that. However, the breads in the

natural leaven chapter were baked and photographed at a restaurant where I work, Locanda Locatelli, the home of our best Italian chef, Giorgio Locatelli. These breads were baked in an electric deck oven, a type some readers will have in their bakeries. The resulting pictures show that the difference between these loaves and the others in the book is not so great, although they are a little better. Good bread is more about dough quality than anything else.

Photographing the book myself was the answer to a problem. So often I have wished for a photographer to be there with me as I baked or worked with other bakers. But budgets don't often stretch to that (bakers are less costly than photographers), and for this book I wanted to show you what I saw, usually with the intimacy that only a solitary traveller can encounter. And the baking clan being what it is, I was accepted as a baker in places where a photographer might have stumbled. The bread was the key, and opened the doors and homes of many extraordinary and talented bakers around Europe. Given the chance, I would write a book about each of them.

In many of the places I visited, home-baking flourished alongside the small independent baker, occasionally in a symbiotic relationship. Bakeries would supply flour, grains, and yeast for home-bakers, and in return the home-bakers would buy bread and sometimes share home-grown ingredients with the bakeries. But always the home-bakers would support the local bakers, buying bread to supplement their effort. I know the effort that goes into a good loaf, and this book doesn't hide the time and thought it takes. So every time I'm in a bakery I remember that, and buy a loaf when I can. If I have too much, then I know I have enough to share.

Ingredients

Cook's notes: weights and measurements

Cook's notes: bakers' percentages

In this book, weights are primarily given in metric, an old and easily understandable system of measurement, and one that helps clarify the reasoning behind the recipe. I beg you to resist any reservations you have about metrication and embrace it as a helpful system. A kilo is a kilo is a kilo wherever you are and that will always hold true, no matter how much kitchen cups and fluid ounces vary. There are imperial fluid ounces and US fluid ounces, Australian cups and US cups, but a gram is the same in Melbourne, Houston or Edinburgh. Our governments insist we use precisely calibrated weighing systems in commercial transactions, yet there is often no clear way of knowing exactly what the units stand for on domestic measuring jugs, cups and spoons. Metric measurement also allows for greater precision when translating very personalized recipes. If a baker's recipe is measured in handfuls, I weigh the quantity their hand can hold in grams to get a precise idea of what the weight will be and thus stay true to the recipe. In this book liquid is measured in grams so that all ingredients can be weighed together in a single jug or bowl.

Many experienced bakers use a system of measurement based on percentages. If the total amount of flour in a recipe equals 100 per cent, then every other ingredient can be described as a percentage of that quantity. These percentages are listed beside the ingredients and are there to help explain the rationale behind the recipe and to enable you to scale up or scale down the recipes as you choose.

Flour

A bag of flour usually contains milled grain from many different types of wheat. Though some types of wheat are all-round winners, these varieties might also be scarce and/or expensive. A single-grain flour might also be better suited to some purposes than others. By sourcing wheat from different farms, or regions, or even countries, the grain merchant can supply the miller with versatile blends.

This is only possible now that choice is actually available. Immersed in 21st-century retail excess, we can barely imagine a world in which the bulk of the population had no such choice, only what could be grown and delivered locally. But once, all life away from the cities was simple and local. After the Industrial Revolution things started to change, and from the mid-19th century onwards the pace of change quickened. Better farming tools, a new chemical industry churning out fertilizers, the scientific analysis of wheat, and the development of faster, more efficient means of transport, all meant that farmers could produce more varieties of grain, in greater volume, and get them to market in the rapidly expanding cities. Ingredients previously scarce or expensive began to be available in larger quantities at an affordable price.

Where a farmer once had a single grain variety, now he had a choice; where a town once had one grain merchant, now there were several. Given this new choice, millers became able to experiment, to produce a single flour with all of the characteristics desirable for breadmaking, and they did this by blending the wheat varieties available. Some varieties helped produce resilient and extensible (stretchy) dough, some a very white or yellow crumb, and some contained high levels of natural sugar in the form of maltose, which gave the finished loaf sweetness and flavour.

Likewise, millers today blend wheat varieties, taking into account the grain colour, strength, and flavour, in order to produce flour that will satisfy their baker customers. Though bakers talk of the supreme importance of the gluten quality, the final characteristics of the flour are determined by many factors and may best be judged by both the overall performance of the flour and the specific purpose it will be used for. Don't judge a flour simply by its protein content.

The farmer and miller grade wheat according to the characteristics that not only identify the variety, but also tell us something of the grain's quality. These characteristics include the colour (red, white or mixed), and the structure (soft, medium or hard). The term "spring wheat" refers to a variety that is planted in March or April and harvested in July or August of the same year. On an organic farm, spring wheat would yield 3½ tonnes of grain per hectare. The term "winter wheat" refers to a variety that is planted in October or November, germinates over the next few weeks, and is harvested the following year, perhaps 10 or 12 days earlier than the spring variety. A typical winter variety, organically farmed, would yield 6 tonnes of grain per hectare of land; almost double the yield from spring wheat.

As farming is a business, farmers need to maximize their yield from each hectare of land. This means farmers may be less likely to plant spring wheat varieties, which don't bring the same financial return – especially if they are supplying customers who view the flour as a cheap, generic commodity. To encourage and support the farming of rare, local, and lower-yielding crops, such as these spring wheats, we must be prepared to pay more for them.

The recipes in this book call for flour from many different grains, as specified in the introduction to the breads. Not all are available at the supermarket; some need to be searched out (a list of stockists is printed on page 190) or ordered in advance. But without the recipes, there won't be the interest. And without the interest, the grains just won't be grown.

Gluten in flour

Gluten is a complex, sticky, elastic protein that is present in the flour from many grains. In wheat flour it is the gluten that traps the carbon dioxide released by the yeasts as they ferment the sugars in the dough, creating a bold, well-risen loaf, and it is the gluten that provides the skeletal structure in the crumb. In rye flour, it is proteins similar to gluten that give the dough its stickiness, but without the elasticity or extensibility of wheat dough.

The protein content listed in the nutritional information on the side of a bag of flour will not tell you the gluten content. The gluten in wheat flour only accounts for up to 80 per cent of the total protein. The other 20 per cent or so is made up mostly of soluble protein, which will thicken when salt is added or when it is baked, adding to the texture of the finished loaf. A small percentage of the protein is insoluble, forming part of the grain structure. But it is the gluten which, when hydrated, forms a complex structure bound together with very small quantities of carbohydrates, fats, and minerals present in the flour.

The gluten is best seen as a continuous network within the dough, which binds lipids (fats) and entraps starch. For this reason, bread has been described as "gluten foam". The gluten itself has no flavour or aroma; these are carried by the starches and lipids in the flour. The recognizable flavour of good bread is created when these starches and fats are combined with bacteria and enzymes found naturally in the flour, or introduced by the yeast or ferment.

The two main constituents of gluten are: gliadin, a sticky substance that helps to bind the gluten into a cohesive compound and contributes to the viscosity and stretchiness of the dough; and glutenin, which gives the dough its strength and resilience. It is variations in the characteristics of the glutenin that account for most of the differences between types of wheat flours. Two flours can have a similar protein content, yet behave vastly differently. Experiment, talk to your miller, and find out which flours you prefer.

Yeast

FRESH YEAST VERSUS DRY ACTIVE YEAST Yeast belongs to the family of organisms known as fungi. When added to a mixture of water and flour, it will use the sugars contained in the flour in order to ferment, releasing carbon dioxide as it does so. This aerates the mixture. When baked, the yeast is killed, but the aeration in the dough remains, giving a light texture to the loaf. The yeast you buy has been grown selectively in order to supply the baker with a pure strain that will multiply quickly at a predictable rate and aerate the dough adequately.

I've found a marked improvement in the results I achieve when baking with fresh yeast. To replicate the results in this book, I would recommend that you seek out and use fresh yeast where required. However, in many instances this is difficult, usually because the demand isn't there to warrant local availability. In many northern European countries, small blocks of fresh yeast weighing 50g are widely available in small supermarkets. This is because more people bake at home in these countries, in addition to supporting their local bakery. If we start to bake more at home, we can demand the same convenience.

When you need to replace the fresh yeast in the recipe with dry active yeast, do the following. Take 25 per cent of the water from a recipe and heat it to 38–40°C. Whisk in the dry yeast (half the weight given for fresh yeast), together with 2–3 tbsp of flour from the total amount. Leave this for 20 minutes, then use in the recipe as if using fresh yeast.

NATURAL LEAVEN VERSUS COMMERCIAL YEAST Prior to the widespread availability of commercially prepared yeast, bakers would leave a mixture of flour and water to ferment, and use this as the source of yeast for their recipe. The yeasts that naturally collect on surfaces and grains multiply more slowly than the commercial strains, produce less carbon dioxide, and prefer cooler temperatures. This method is increasingly practised by bakers who want to re-establish old flavours and textures by using techniques shaped over hundreds of years. By doing so they are creating breads that sell very well to a public increasingly disenchanted with the bland taste of mass-market foods.

The adage here must be to bake with what you have; make the best of what is around you. For some, there is no choice in their minds but to use a natural leaven as the sole ferment within a dough. For others, this is akin to witchcraft, and a madness in an age of convenience. To my mind, a beautiful loaf, wrought with care and consideration, must be the aim; and in trying to write a useful book, I have come to understand that for each reader this means something different. How you get to the end loaf does matter, and the choice you make must be honest and heartfelt. If you have never tried baking with the slower yeasts, then try at least once – or more. Through practice you will begin to understand the simplicity of natural leaven baking, and how its construction, appearance and aroma will echo through the loaf.

BLOCKS OF FRESH YEAST in the Ukraine, Russia, and Sweden, sold in small 50g units for home use.

Sea salt and malted grains

Sometimes the ingredients we most want to use are not in a form that is best suited to baking. Yet somehow when we are shown them again in a perfect, processed form, they are less alluring. How difficult is it to prepare ingredients ourselves and make them suitable for our needs? Not very, and the results are sometimes preferable.

SALT There is a type of grey sea salt that is available from health-food stores in continental Europe, though less readily available in the UK. This salt is one of the things I return with when I travel. It is made up of coarse, hard, roundish crystals that don't dissolve easily in water. If this is not available, look for the purest salt you can find, without anti-caking agents, and go to the bother of grinding it yourself. The best and easiest way is with a large mortar and pestle. Weigh the salt in a small cup, then tip this into the mortar and grind it in a circular motion with the pestle.

SALT QUANTITY IN RECIPES My view is that, for the majority of bread recipes, the salt is an integral part of the loaf, and that bread usually needs to be considered a sodium-rich foodstuff, almost like salt-cured fish. Salt is part of the taste and enhances the flavour of the grain. But we eat to live, or should do if we respect the body that carries us, and it is right and proper that we vary our diet according to what our needs are. Please do vary or omit the salt used in the recipes here. We are told that even a small reduction in our dietary sodium intake will benefit us, and many of our processed foods have a hidden sodium (salt) content where you wouldn't expect it to be – in breakfast cereal, for example. For children, two slices of bread can sometimes equal their recommended daily sodium requirement (which is surprisingly small). So use salt respectfully.

MALT Malt occurs naturally in minute amounts in wheat grains. If the grain is left to sprout, enzymes will convert starch into maltose, which will be used by the seedling for growth. If the sprouted grain is dried, gently roasted and ground, the resulting powder can be mixed with the flour to add colour and flavour to the final loaf, and will be fermented by the yeast. Throughout Europe, malt has been traditionally and widely used in bread baking, and some old water mills still have a roasting oven for the toasting of sprouted grains. It is, however, in the world of beer and brewing where the full range of malt colours and strengths can be seen. A home-brewing shop, if there is one near you, can supply a range of natural malted grains, and these simply require grinding in order to be used; a coffee or spice grinder (the kind of accessory you usually find tucked in the box when you buy a blender) is the perfect tool. Measure out the weight of malt needed, then tip it into the spice or coffee grinder and in seconds it will be reduced to a powder that can be mixed with the flour.

Mixing, shaping, & baking

Mixing the dough

Through necessity and perhaps in an attempt to emulate the gentler mixing of the artisan bakers' preferred twin-arm mixers, I have evolved a hand-kneading method that borders on no-kneading. I haven't invented or discovered anything; as I read and talked with other bakers, I realized that others have also nudged towards a similar conclusion.

For me, it started years ago, when I worked as a pastry chef in a restaurant and had several different bread dough recipes on the go at once. At the same time I was also racing around trying to get ice-cream churned, two tarts baked, peaches roasted, and rock-hard pears simmered to tender perfection, while staying calm, organized and ever-willing to respond with a polite "*Oui*, chef". And yep, I'd forget the bread.

Well, not exactly forget, but I'd get so caught up in other work that I'd start mixing one dough, then leave it for 10–15 minutes while I mixed the next one; then cover and leave that while I raced downstairs to check the ice-cream machine. Then I'd go back upstairs to quickly knead the dough again. And I'd realise that, during the wait, something remarkable had happened to the dough. Within seconds of returning to knead the dough again, it felt smooth and resilient. I'd cover the dough, leave it another 10–15 minutes, race around doing other things, and when I returned and began to knead the dough once more it appeared even smoother and more elastic. It was as if it had been perfectly kneaded for 10 minutes.

Then I tried another variation. Rather than kneading on a flour-dusted work-surface, which always slightly reduced the moisture content of the dough, I tried lightly oiling the work-surface each time. This stopped the dough from sticking, but made certain that the recipe stayed true to the carefully crafted percentages of water-to-flour that gave the loaf its particular crumb structure.

For the last 10 years this has been my preferred method of mixing bread dough in small quantities (under 5kg). It is better than by machine for small quantities, and great even in small bakeries, when only a few loaves are needed.

PRE-MIXING WITHOUT LEAVENING, AND DELAYING THE ADDITION OF SALT The technique described above had, in fact, been investigated years earlier. In his studies in the early 1970s, the French bakery writer Professor Raymond Calvel found that the full hydration of flour and its gluten occurs over time rather than instantaneously. After mixing flour with water, a short pause of 10–20 minutes allows the particles of flour to swell with moisture, and gives the protein strands of gliadin and glutenin time to hydrate. If the addition of leaven, which is already fully hydrated, is delayed until after this has occurred, the effect on both the dough's resilience, extensibility, and crumb structure is pronounced. If you delay the addition of salt as well, which has a tightening effect on the gluten, then the benefit of this process (known as autolysis) is amplified. For the recipes in this book, I have not delayed the addition of leaven or salt, but once you are comfortable with your technique, then do so.

KNEADING ON AN OILED SURFACE
1 Lightly oil a small, clean patch of work-surface.
2 Scrape the dough out of the bowl and on to the oiled surface.
3 Knead for 5–10 seconds. Stop kneading before the dough absorbs the oil and sticks to the surface.
4 Flip the dough over and leave to rest.

MANIPULATING THE DOUGH DURING THE INITIAL RISE
This is common practice among artisan bakers – it elongates the bubbles formed by the yeast and so changes the dough's handling properties.
1 Stretch the dough out on the work-surface and pat it out lightly into a rectangle.
2 Fold the dough back in on itself by thirds, first in one direction and then in the other.

MIXING DOUGH BY HAND Take the measured amount of liquid and stir into it the yeast or natural leaven, breaking up any lumps. Weigh the dry ingredients. Stir the dry ingredients with the liquid quickly and smoothly. The aim is to try and get the liquid evenly mixed at first, and since the flour will begin to clump as soon as it makes contact with the liquid, the quicker you can mix this the better. Dig your hands right down to the bottom of the bowl to make sure there is neither a clump of flour, nor a pool of liquid, sitting there. Then squidge the dough through the fingers of your hand so that there are few lumps left. Scrape whatever dough is sticking to your hands back into the bowl, then cover the dough and leave for 10 minutes (or whatever time is suggested in the recipe).

Lightly oil a small, clean patch of work-surface. Scrape the dough from the bowl out on to the oiled surface and knead briefly for 5–10 seconds, stopping before the dough absorbs the oil and sticks. Cover the dough with a cloth, and quickly clean the bowl out with warm water (this will help keep the dough free from stray bits that could harden on the inner surface of the bowl). Dry and lightly oil the bowl, then lift the dough from the work surface and replace it in the bowl. Cover with a cloth and leave for 10 minutes (or whatever time is suggested in the recipe).

Each time you knead the dough, it should be a conscious and deliberate act rather than a frantic aerobic activity. Initially you are looking to mix the moisture through the dough evenly, watching out for any lumps that need breaking with your fingers and combining the ingredients into one smooth, uniform, and cohesive mass.

Now repeat the kneading once more. Spread a little more oil on the work-surface, then remove the dough from the bowl and begin to knead it gently once more, for 10–15 seconds. You will notice at once that the dough seems smoother and more resilient. Also, as the yeast cells release carbon dioxide into the dough, these bubbles will become stretched and elongated during the repeated kneading, which will result in the crumb of the loaf having an open texture.

TURNING THE DOUGH It has become common for artisan bakers, both in commercial bakeries and at home, to manipulate the dough during the initial rise. This involves stretching the dough out on the work surface, patting it out lightly into a rectangle, then folding it back in on itself by thirds, first in one direction and then the other. This gentle stretching elongates the bubbles formed by the fermenting yeast and in doing so changes the handling properties of dough with a high (68 per cent plus) water content. Much like the strength that is created in a cellular foam such as a whipped meringue, the surface tension that each bubble creates helps the dough to sit upright rather than spread in a flowing mass on the bench.

If I'm making a dough with a high percentage of water, I first place it in an oiled and lipped tray that is large enough to cope with the inevitable flow of the dough. Then, as the dough is gently stretched and folded during the initial fermentation, it appears to gain resilience as the texture becomes more open. By the end, and before its final weighing and shaping, this liquid dough has transformed into a manageable and workable mass.

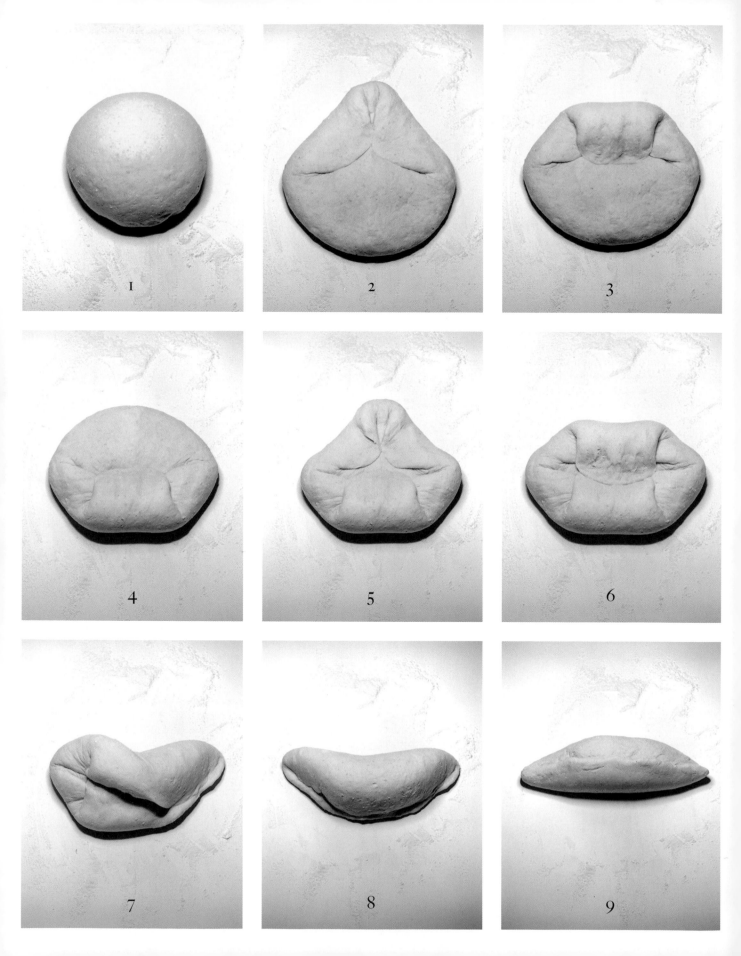

Shaping the dough

SHAPING A BATON (1) Shape the dough into a ball, cover and leave to rest for 10 minutes. This gets the dough into a neat, even shape first, and helps to ensure that the final oval shape is symmetrical.

(2) Pat the dough out into a flat oval, seam-side-up. Imagine the piece of dough has four curved sides. Take the two sides furthest from you and fold them in to the centre, pressing them down well so that they seal.

(3) Then take the point that has formed and fold that in to the centre, pressing it down to seal it well.

(4) Next, flip the dough around 180°.

(5/6) Repeat with the other side. This flipping helps to keep the dough shape even. Then flip the dough around once more.

(7) Fold the dough evenly in half towards you.

(8) Seal both edges together with the heel of your hand.

(9) Roll the dough back and forward on the work surface, pressing down ever so slightly with your hands so that any trapped air in the folded shape is forced out towards the ends. If you increase the pressure placed by the outer part of both hands, you can give the loaf pointed ends. Place the dough seam-side-up on a floured cloth.

SHAPING A BALL Place the piece of dough, with the smoothest side facing downward, on to the oiled or lightly floured surface. With your right hand (if you are right-handed), start folding the edges of the piece of dough in toward the centre, then hold each in place with the thumb of the left hand while you rotate the dough and fold again eight times, creating a roughly octagonal piece of dough with all of the edges pinched in towards the centre. Now flip the dough over. Without too much flour or oil on the surface, drag the dough from left to right (if you are right-handed), rotating it clockwise but forcing it to stick ever so slightly to the work-surface.

Think about this. What is happening is that the slight adhesion of the dough to the work-surface pulls the outer surface of the dough. Then, as you are also pushing and slowly rotating the dough across the work-surface, this causes the outer surface of the dough to be pulled very tight. This is exactly what you want. No more spinning the dough on a heavily floured surface; let it stick just slightly as you push and rotate it gently so that the outer surface becomes taut and smooth. Do this two or three times, but no more as the dough would then start to tear. Place the dough seam-side-up on a floured cloth.

SHAPING A STICK Initially shape the dough into a baton (as above), cover and then leave to rest for 10 minutes. Starting at one end, fold the dough in half once more while at the same time sealing the edges together with the heel of your hand. Finally, roll the dough back and forward on the work-surface, pressing down ever so slightly with your hands so that any trapped air in the folded shape is forced out towards the ends and the dough is gradually stretched into a long stick. If you increase the pressure placed by the outer part of both hands, you can give the stick pointed ends. Place the dough seam-side-up on a floured cloth.

Slashing the dough

Baking the loaf

In theory, you could ensure that your loaf rises to its fullest extent prior to baking. Then it would only expand a little in the oven and achieve a perfect, unbroken crust. But in reality this is not only difficult to achieve but also undesirable because, should there be an unexpected delay the moment before your loaf goes into the oven, the whole baking session could be ruined as a result. Don't take this risk.

Instead, bakers have turned this problem into a beautiful tradition. If the loaf goes into the oven with a cut across the surface before the dough has fully expanded (or when the dough is "young"), then it will rise and tear along that cut. This deliberate slicing through the skin of the dough ensures that expansion will break through where the least surface tension exists.

To slash the dough, get a very sharp blade from a craft shop (or use a safety razor blade). Being especially careful not to cut yourself, hold the blade at an angle, and with a swift action slash the surface of the dough. If this troubles you, then you can also clip at the surface of the dough with a pair of scissors.

It is worth investing in a few pieces of equipment. First, get an oven thermometer. Just before starting this book I checked my oven at home. The dial said 220°C; the thermometer said 180°C. Bread will still bake adequately in a lower temperature oven, but it will take longer to get a good crust, bake paler and look less dramatic. If your oven cannot reach 220°C/425°F/gas mark 7, just increase the baking time.

Modern domestic ovens are designed to do best what we do most often: reheat food. They're not really designed for baking, but aim to keep food dry and crisp, which is just what we don't want. An Aga is an exception, as it doesn't let much moisture escape during baking. Great for us bakers (not so good for ready-meal peddlers). For the first 10 minutes of baking, the loaf needs to expand to it fullest extent and its surface needs to stay soft and supple in order to do this. A moist environment enables this to happen. To overcome the dryness of modern ovens, invest in a refillable fine-misting water spray. A quick spray on to the cut surface of the dough just before it goes into the oven, and again after 5 minutes, seems to help produce a dramatic tear in the loaf. This can be done in addition to ice-cubes tossed into a hot tray, or water sprayed around the sides of the oven just before the bread goes in.

If you are using a baking stone, place that in the oven and allow it to heat up before baking. This helps retain the heat in the oven, which is useful if you have one of these modern domestic ovens that is woefully lacking in insulation and works somewhat better as a kitchen heater. A hot, thick metal tray will also act as a baking surface. Most of the recipes in this book assume the reader wants to place the bread on a cold tray and then place that tray in the hot oven. A better result will be achieved if you upturn the loaf on to a thin semolina-dusted board (what bakers call a peel or a pizza shovel), and then deposit the loaf on to the hot stone or tray. When cold dough is placed on a hot stone, there is a sudden outward push from the steam created inside the dough, which improves both the loaf's internal texture and boldness. It is only recently that research groups worldwide, through the use of the latest scientific measurements, are beginning to understand this ancient process; for example, by the thermal imaging of baking loaves done by Professor Laurie Hall at Cambridge University.

The
natural
leaven

Creating a leaven

Leavened bread is bread that has risen, puffed with gasses that create a cellular network of pockets throughout the dough. These gasses are produced by fermentation, a process whereby an organism, in this case one of the Saccharomyces strain of fungi we know as "yeast", releases carbon dioxide as it assimilates and uses the sugars present in the dough. Bacteria can also ferment sugars, and are often present together with yeast when fermentation occurs.

Yeast might be found on the surface of grains such as wheat, or on the skin of fruits rich in sugars, or in a spoonful of an already fermenting mixture. When these are mixed with fresh water and flour, the yeasts will slowly multiply and ferment. Some bacteria will give the leaven its distinctive sour aroma and taste – as with the bacterium Lactobacillus Sanfrancisco, which has been isolated by scientists, and to which the

remarkable bright flavour of the San Francisco sourdough is attributed.

A simple mixture of flour and water, stirred and left in a warm place, may ferment and produce an active leaven. In Sweden, I mixed locally milled rye flour with water, and refreshed it with additional flour and water daily. By day five, it was bubbling with fermentation and the actual leaven is shown in the picture below. But I haven't always been so lucky. The recipe that I have relied on in the past, which is shown on the following pages, contains two other ingredients: raisins, since it is likely that they will harbour yeast on their surface; and yoghurt, because it contains lactic bacteria. All the breads using leaven in this book have been made with a leaven initiated from this recipe.

This recipe, as well as samples of the leaven it produces, was sent to the National Collection of Yeast Cultures (NCYC) in Norwich. They followed the recipe, and by day five the fermentation had begun. But we were curious about exactly which organisms had caused it. So the ingredients were streaked out on standard YM agar plates to look for yeast or bacterial colonies. After one week at 25°C, the sample from the raisins produced the largest amount of yeast, with a small amount also being found in the wheat flour. The yoghurt, and to a much lesser extent the rye flour, produced only bacterial colonies. It is speculated that these bacteria multiply in the initial mixture and alter it by breaking down the flour and lowering the pH until the yeast gradually multiply and take over. A leaven given to me in Denmark by Eva Hauch (see page 72), and reputed by Eva to be more than 100 years old, was also tested. This contained many different yeast and bacterial cells. It is possible that leaven might develop a complex variety of yeast and bacterial cultures according to what it is refreshed with over a long period of time.

The yeasts in your leaven will initially multiply very slowly. By adding fresh water and flour to the leaven once or twice a day, the chances of a strong and healthy fermentation are increased. Ideally, after the sixth day onward, each new addition (or "refreshment") should be four or five times the quantity that is in the jar. Do this, and the yeasts in the leaven will multiply at an optimum rate in the reduced pH, will stay healthy, and will produce enough carbon dioxide to aerate your bread successfully.

Leaven recipe

Here is a recipe, or perhaps more correctly, a set of ingredients and steps, that will promote fermentation in a leaven of flour and water. Though fermentation will occur simply with flour and water, I have added a few other ingredients that I like and have grown accustomed to. (I have also tried making the leaven solely with organic rye flour, using slightly less that the suggested amount of white flour; it worked a treat.) I photographed every step of making the leaven each morning in my home kitchen so that you can see exactly what the process should look like.

DAY 1

150g water at 20°C

2 rounded tsp rye flour

2 rounded tsp strong white flour

2 rounded tsp currants or raisins

2 rounded tsp live low-fat yoghurt

Mix all the ingredients in a 500ml Kilner jar. Cover and leave at room temperature (approx. 20°C) for 24 hours.

DAY 2

50g water at 20°C

2 rounded tsp rye flour

2 rounded tsp strong white flour

By this stage there will be no perceptible change, though some yeasts will have multiplied. The surface will look shiny as the solids separate from the water and sink down in the jar. Stir the above ingredients into the leaven, starting with the water, followed by the dry ingredients. Cover and leave again at room temperature (approx. 20°C) for 24 hours.

DAY 3

100g water at 20°C

4 rounded tsp strong white flour

4 rounded tsp rye flour

By this time the raisins (or currants) will have started to break down and you will notice a coffee coloured ring around them as they sit in the mixture. Also, there will be the odd pin hole of fermentation on the surface. Add the water, stir well to combine, then add the flours and stir again. The mixture will look frothy, but this is simply from the stirring. Nearly there. Cover and leave again at room temperature (approx. 20°C) for 24 hours.

DAY 4

100g water at 20°C

125g strong white flour

By this time the froth of fermentation should be beginning, though there will be only the vaguest hint of acidity in the aroma. Remove and discard three-quarters of the mixture. Add the water and stir well. Pour the mixture through a tea strainer to remove the raisins (or currants), then put the strained liquid back into the Kilner jar. Add the flour and stir again. Cover and leave at room temperature (approx. 20°C) for 24 hours.

DAY 5

100g water at 20°C

125g strong white flour

The fermentation should be clearly evident, and the aroma starting to become acid. You can notice this the moment you remove the lid from the jar, though it disappears quickly. Remove and discard three-quarters of the mixture. Add the water and stir well so that the mixture thins evenly. Stir in the flour so that you have a thick paste. I prefer to keep the refreshment slightly heavier on flour than water, as this slows the fermentation and stops the leaven rising and falling too quickly. Cover and leave again at room temperature (approx. 20°C) for 24 hours.

DAY 6 ONWARDS Take the lid off the jar, and you will see the mixture bubbling. Each day, as you remove some leaven for baking, replacing it with an equivalent amount of flour and water, the aroma of the leaven will become stronger and more sharply acidic.

DAY 1 Mix water, flour, raisins, and yoghurt together in the proportions stated in the recipe on page 25, in a small Kilner jar and leave at room temperature for 24 hours.

DAY 2 The surface should look shiny. Add water and flour in the proportions stated in the recipe on page 25, and again leave at room temperature for 24 hours.

DAY 3 The raisins will have started to break down. Again add water and flour in the proportions stated in the recipe on page 25, and leave at room temperature for 24 hours.

DAY 4 By now the froth of fermentation should be beginning. Again add water and flour in the proportions stated in the recipe on page 25, pour the mixture through a strainer, and return the strained liquid to the jar. Leave for 24 hours.

DAY 5 By now the fermentation should be clearly evident and the aroma acidic. Discard three-quarters of the mixture. Add water in the proportions stated in the recipe on page 25, stir, then add and stir in flour. Leave for another 24 hours.

TO STORE THE LEAVEN FOR USE If used regularly, some bakers keep their leaven at room (or bakery) temperature, others keep it chilled at 12–15°C. Regular refreshment, for at least two days prior to baking, is needed to keep the leaven active and in prime condition.

TO STORE THE LEAVEN FOR USE ANOTHER TIME If you want to store the leaven, without using it, for longer periods, this will force some of the yeast cells to become dormant and some to die. Leave the leaven covered and undisturbed at the back of the refrigerator (at 4°C). As it sits unrefreshed, the leaven will separate into a dark coffee-coloured liquid, which sits on top, and a solid grey mixture, which lies at the bottom of the jar.

TO REVIVE THE LEAVEN Carefully take 1–2 tsp of the grey putty-like leaven from the bottom of the stored jar, and stir this into a fresh quantity of 100g (80%) water and 125g (100%) white flour. Leave at room temperature (approx. 20°C) for 24 hours, then remove three-quarters and refresh once more with 100g of water and 125g white flour. Leave for another 24 hours, by which time the mixture should have fermented again. For the next refreshment, add sufficient fresh flour and water, in proportions of 80% water to 100% flour, to make enough leaven for your baking. Stir well, cover for 24 hours, and use in baking the following day.

ABOVE: DAY 6 Take the lid off the jar and you will see the mixture bubbling. Each day, as you continue to remove leaven for baking, replace it with an equivalent amount of flour and water.
LEFT: The unrefreshed leaven after two months stored in a refrigerator.

White leaven bread

If soda makes a quick bread, then this recipe, using the leaven made on the previous pages, is a very, very slow bread. The yeast you have cultured has multiplied slowly, together with lactic bacteria, to create a distinctive, sour taste to the crumb. The extended kneading during the initial fermentation, or rise, will help to stretch the minute air bubbles released by the yeast, enlarging them to create a web of exaggerated holes throughout the crumb. I've suggested times to help give an indication of how long the process will take, from that first drop of water hitting the flour until the unbaked loaf finally enters the hot oven.

TIP Clear time to make this and the other loaves in this chapter. You can stretch the times by altering the temperatures, for example by mixing the dough at night, leaving it in the refrigerator overnight, removing it in the morning and letting it return to 16–18°C, together with a light kneading (or by turning the dough, see page 19). All breads can only be made if they suit the time you have available, whether in a bakery or in your home.

200g white leaven (see pages 25–27) at 18°C (40%)
325g cold water at 16°C (65%)
500g strong white flour (100%)

1½ tsp fine sea salt (2%)
optional: 1½ tsp ground malted grains (see page 39) (1.5%)
semolina, for dusting the tray or peel

8.00AM In a large bowl, whisk the leaven with the water (and ground malted grains, if using). Add the flour and salt, and stir together with your hands until you have a soft, sticky mass. The dough temperature should be about 20°C. Scrape any remaining dough from your hands, cover the bowl and leave for 10 minutes. Wash and dry your hands, removing stuck bits of dough from your fingers.

8.10AM Remove the dough from the bowl and place on a lightly oiled (with corn or olive oil) or flour-dusted work-surface. Knead the dough for 10–15 seconds. While this initially seems a short knead, it is still important to work the dough thoroughly. I find by kneading the dough 12 times, rotating it in quarter turns, this can be achieved. Shape the dough into a ball, and leave covered on the work-surface. Clean and dry the bowl, and give it a light rub inside with oil.

8.20AM Knead the dough for 10–15 seconds, shape into a ball, and then place the dough back in the bowl. Cover and leave at room temperature (20°C) for 10 minutes.

8.30AM Knead the dough for 10–15 seconds, shape into a ball, and then place the dough back in the bowl. Cover and leave for 30 minutes.

9.00AM Knead the dough for 10–15 seconds, shape into a ball, and then place the dough back in the bowl. Cover and leave for 1 hour.

10.00AM Knead the dough for 10–15 seconds, shape into a ball, and then place the dough back in the bowl. Cover and leave for 1 hour.

11.00AM Knead the dough for 10–15 seconds, shape into a ball, and then place the dough back in the bowl. Cover and leave for 2 hours.

1.00PM Divide the dough into two pieces, each roughly 500g in weight. Shape each piece into a ball, cover, and leave on the work-surface for 15 minutes.

1.15PM Rub two clean tea-towels with flour, then use them to line two bowls (20cm wide), or use flour-dusted, linen-lined baskets if you have them (though expensive, they last a long time). Dust the work-surface with flour. Shape the dough once more into balls, and then place each seam side up in the flour-dusted cloths sitting inside the bowls. Cover the upper surface with a cloth, and leave at room temperature (20°C) until almost doubled in height – around 4½ hours.

5.30PM Preheat the oven to 220°C/425°F/gas mark 7. As naturally leavened loaves rise much more slowly, there isn't the same urgency when it comes to time to bake the loaf. Dust an oven tray, or a peel if you are using an oven stone, with semolina. Upturn one loaf on to the tray (or peel), and with a sharp blade cut a circle around the circumference of the loaf. Spray the top of the loaf with water, and bake for 50–70 minutes. Cool on a wire rack. Bake the remaining loaf using the same technique.

This loaf uses a mix of white, wholewheat and rye flour, and this recipe could make use of any other grain flours (60% white to 40% other flour) so long as the white flour stays dominant. The method is almost identical to the white leaven bread on page 28, but the result is quite different, with a dark, nutty, sour taste to the crust and crumb.

The mill loaf

500g white leaven (50%) (see pages 25–27)

550g water at 20°C (55%)

optional: 1 tsp ground malted grains (0.5%)
    (see page 39)

600g white flour (60%)

300g wholewheat flour (30%)

100g rye flour (10%)

2½ tsp fine sea salt (2%)

8.00AM In a large bowl, whisk the leaven with the water (and malt, if using). Add the flours and salt, and stir with your hands until you have a soft, sticky mass. The dough temperature should be about 20°C. Scrape any dough from your hands, cover the bowl, and leave for 10 minutes. Wash and dry your hands and any utensils.

8.10AM Remove the dough from the bowl and place on a lightly oiled (with corn or olive oil) or flour-dusted work-surface. Knead the dough for 10–15 seconds, or 12 times, rotating it in quarter turns. Shape the dough into a ball, and leave covered on the work-surface for 10 minutes. Clean the bowl, and give it a light rub with oil.

8.20AM Knead the dough for 10–15 seconds, shape into a ball, then place back in the bowl. Cover and leave at room temperature (about 20°C) for a 10 minutes.

8.30AM Knead the dough for 10–15 seconds, shape into a ball, then place back in the bowl. Cover and leave for 30 minutes.

9.00AM Knead the dough for 10–15 seconds, shape into a ball, then place back in the bowl. Cover and leave for 1 hour.

10.00AM Knead the dough for 10–15 seconds, shape into a ball, then place back in the bowl. Cover and leave for 1 hour.

11.00AM Dust the work-surface with flour. Divide the dough into two equal pieces. Gently knead each piece for 10 seconds and round into a ball. Cover and leave for 10 minutes on the work-surface, to give the dough time to relax. Rub a clean tea-towel with flour, so the dough doesn't stick to it, and lay across a large tray.

11.15AM Sit a ball of dough seam-side-upwards on the floured work-surface (see page 20). Pat it flat with your hands, then take the left and right sides furthest from you and fold them in towards the centre by 2cm, making a triangular point. Take that point and fold it inwards to the centre, pressing it down to seal. Rotate the dough 180°, then repeat with the other side. Rotate the dough again, back to the start position.

If you're right-handed, fold the dough in half towards you, starting at the right-hand end, sealing it with the heel of your right hand while holding and folding it with your left. Roll the shaped loaf with both hands, pressing slightly more with the heel of each hand to give the ends a point. Place the dough seam-side-up on the cloth. Fold and pull the cloth up the sides of the loaf (if using a linen-lined basket, just place the dough seam-side upwards inside). Repeat with the remaining dough and sit this next to the first piece, separated by the cloth. Cover with a cloth, and leave at room temperature (20°C) until almost doubled in height – about 4 hours.

3.30–4.30PM Preheat the oven to 220°C/425°F/gas mark 7. Dust an oven tray, or a peel if you are using an oven stone, with semolina. Upturn one loaf on to the tray and cut two slashes across it. Spray the top of the loaf with water and bake for 50–70 minutes. Cool on a wire rack. Bake the remaining loaf using the same technique.

Sour 100% rye bread

This is one of those legendary breads that become easier once you understand the method used. Jan Hedh, the esteemed Swedish baker, who has taught and inspired most of the new breed of artisan bakers in that country and is an inspiration throughout Scandinavia, enlightened me on how to work with and manipulate rye flour. The mixture of almost boiling water with a small amount of rye flour, used as both an addition to the dough and a wash over the exterior of the loaf, gives elasticity to both the crust and crumb. As it was traditional in rural societies to cook grains as a mash with water, you can imagine leftovers finding their way into the baker's mix.

TIP For the gelatinized mixture, it is worth noting that different temperatures of hot water produce different results. Try two different mixes, one with the water at 90°C and one with the water at 80°C, and see which you prefer. Use fine rye flour or, if you have trouble finding it, sift coarse rye flour and save the rye bran for dressing the loaf or dusting your proving baskets.

FOR THE GELATINIZED RYE MIX:
240g boiling water (400%)
60g rye flour (100%)

FOR THE DOUGH:
200g rye leaven at 21°C (67%)

50g cold water at 19°C (17%)
300g hot gelatinized rye mix (100%)
300g fine rye flour (100%)
1 tsp fine sea salt (2%)

FOR THE GELATINIZED RYE MIX Cool the boiling water until it reaches 90°C. Quickly whisk in the rye flour trying to avoid too many lumps forming. Cover the bowl and leave for 1 hour (or up to 24 hours). This produces the gelatinized rye mixture that will give the crumb of the loaf some elasticity.

FOR THE DOUGH Make a rye leaven using the recipe for making a leaven (see pages 25–27) but substituting rye flour for white flour at each step. Or take some of your white starter and refresh that using solely rye flour and water for a few days. But remember that rye flour needs more liquid to reach the same consistency as a batter made with white flour.

Whisk the rye leaven into the cold water, then whisk in the gelatinized rye mix (saving 1–2 tbsp to brush over the loaf). Stir this with the dry ingredients until you have a soft sticky paste. Tip this dough out on to a lightly oiled (with corn or olive oil) work-surface and knead gently into a ball. Shape the dough into a baton (see page 21). Place the loaf seam-side-up on a floured cloth, pulling the cloth up around the dough to hold its shape (or use a dusted proving basket). Leave to rise at room temperature for 5 hours, or until the loaf has almost doubled in size.

Preheat the oven to 210°C/410°F/gas mark 6½. Carefully upturn the loaf on to a tray and brush with the gelatinized rye mixture. Spray the loaf lightly with water, and bake for 50 minutes, spraying the loaf again after the first 5 minutes. Leave to cool on a wire rack. When cold, wrap in kitchen baking parchment, tied well with string, and leave for a day before slicing.

Russia

If you are to believe everything you hear and read, Moscow is entering a golden moment, comparable to Berlin in the early 1970s. Old ways sit bang up against big-time modern-living, as restauranteurs and chefs, designers and architects, try to claim a piece of the easy money. The baguette and the croissant, those early warning markers of infringing western values, are starting to appear in truck stops and cafés. But if you look carefully, there are still remarkable breads around, baked using methods and ingredients unusual to us. The likelihood is, however, that these will disappear before people learn to value and preserve them.

Nina Vladimirovna Gorkovenko teaches at Yasnaya Poliana, Tolstoy's grand house in Tula, about 200 miles to the south of Moscow. The place has been preserved as a weekend attraction for Russians, and her job is to teach and demonstrate old ways to groups of visiting children. This is a sort of baking theatre, an enactment of a life that faded around the 1960s, when the sudden proliferation of state-run bakeries started to provide bread for most people.

We sit in a two-roomed wooden house to which Tolstoy would retreat to write, in a building similar to Nina's childhood home. The main room contains the oven, a large beast covered in white tiles, which served both to warm the family and to cook on. Above it is a sleeping platform, a few feet below the wooden ceiling, where the family would have slept together. Underneath the oven is a small space to dry the wood, where the chickens slept at

THIS PAGE, CLOCKWISE FROM TOP LEFT: a braise of rabbit cooked in sour cream, pickled mushrooms and cucumbers; a horse-pulled sledge over snow-covered grain fields; the front of Tolstoy's *izba*; food historian Galina Ivanovna Poskrebysheva; a traditional Uzbekistan bread.
OPPOSITE PAGE, CLOCKWISE FROM TOP LEFT: the hands of Nina Vladimirovna Gorkovenko; chickens in the snow; Andrei Stephanovich Peryakin holding the wheat loaf; wheat and rye loaves rising in a pan at Andrei's house; Claudia Alexandrovna; risen wheat dough being scraped into the pan; Farkhat and Saodat; a wheat loaf in the wood-fired oven; CENTRE, LEFT TO RIGHT: sheets of *matzah* (a dry unleavened bread); the wheat loaf. OVERLEAF: The path to Tolstoy's house; coriander rye at Galina's restaurant.

night. In a corner opposite the oven is the traditional icon, an image of the Virgin Mary in a gilded wooden frame. The front windows face into the curved path of the winter sun that moves low across the horizon.

We are baking together so that I can learn to prepare the traditional oven and watch Nina mix the dough, my hand on a wooden table. "Both my mother and my grandmother used to make dark rye bread each week, and wheat bread on special occasions," said Nina. "I'd help them bake the bread then. There was no other option, as there were no small bakeries, nor anywhere to buy bread. We would grow rye and wheat, and grind it at the collective's mill. Every two or three days my mother would bake six or seven loaves – round loaves each a foot wide by five or six inches high.

"We'd use water if we had water, or milk, or even juice from the cucumber pickle or a little cabbage brine. And if we ran out of bread, we'd get some from our neighbours. In Russia, there are very few people who wouldn't share their bread with you. But, you know, I remember that we were so very happy when we could buy bread. Baking bread was hard work but I think that, like the kneading of the dough, the effort gave people resilience."

Farkhat, a chef in Moscow, and his wife Saodat are a young Uzbek couple living in a old state housing block near the centre of Moscow. They left Tashkent, known as "the city of bread", to find work, leaving their four-year-old daughter behind with their parents. Together we are baking two breads, one a hat-shaped disc of almost unleavened bread and the other a fried flat bread with a dough mixed with onions and larded with small chunks of beef fat, which melt during the cooking, making the texture slightly flaky and oily. "When a young man in Uzbekistan leaves his family and goes to war," Saodat tells me as she shapes a disc of dough into the round, hat-shaped loaf on the table, "he takes a bite from the crust and his father will hang the loaf on the wall as a charm to help him return home safely. So if he returns, he will eat the remaining bread."

I travelled out to the very edges of Moscow, on a three-hour drive through snow-fields, in an old Russian army vehicle, until I reached a little huddle of cottages. At one end is the small, wooden home of Claudia Alexandrovna, the 79-year-old *babushka* (grandmother) who still helps her family bake bread. The leaven was mixed the day before, then mixed into a wheat loaf early the next morning, to be baked in an old saucepan alongside two small rye loaves in oblong bread tins. We wrap the dough-laden tins in thick cloths and travel up to the house of Andrei Stephanovich Peryakin, the godfather to her son Pavel. Andrei had built his own house, a large beautiful wooden home with stables for chickens and rabbits, and inside is a big wood-fired oven in which we'd bake. After the loaves had cooled, we ate a feast of chickens cooked in cream, pickled wild mushrooms, and large fat cucumbers in brine, washed down with sloe vodka made with berries from the garden soaked in grain spirit.

Back in Moscow, I went to visit Galina Ivanovna Poskrebysheva, a respected Russian food writer whose books sell over a million copies per edition. She has a small restaurant where forgotten regional foods are reconstructed and promoted. I asked Galina about the rise in government bakeries in the 1960s. She explained how, since bread was a staple, the government had long tried to make people healthy through maintaining its quality. Every region in Russia had its own bread, made from the local grain, and to make the state bread, government officers collected samples and recipes from each region and used them as the model for their production.

Galina asked a waiter in her restaurant to bring us a slice of one of the regional breads made by her baker Gennady Ivanov. This bread came from a 200-year-old recipe found in the State archives. The whole grain, including the husks, has been left to sprout, then pounded into a paste and mixed with a natural leaven. The taste is sweet and grassy, more vegetable than grain.

"But the bread that is made now, over the past few years, has gotten much worse," she says, somewhat angrily. "Before, the government looked after the bakeries. But after *perestroika*, the government allowed companies to come in and take over the bakeries. Now profit rather than quality is the aim."

White maize and wheat loaf

Corn is found in many different varieties and colours, from a deep rusty purple through golden yellow and white. Though the paler corn makes less visually appetizing polenta, it isn't lacking in flavour and gives a good crunch to the crust of this loaf. The combination of leaven and whey helps the loaf rise quickly and tastes delicious. Either get whey by straining yoghurt or curds through muslin, or save the briny liquid that you find in a packet of mozzarella (and cut the quantity of salt in the recipe by a third).

TIP If you can't find white maize, any other colour will work just fine. Try making curds and whey by mixing a little natural or vegetarian rennet with warm milk, leaving it to stand for 1 hour, then straining it through muslin overnight. Lightly salt the curds, mix with a few chopped fresh herbs, then pack into a earthenware pot. Serve as you would any soft cheese.

230g white leaven at 20°C (46%)
  (see pages 25–27)
325g whey (or yoghurt and water to
  make up the quantity) at 20°C (65%)

300g Italian "00" flour (60%)
100g strong wholewheat flour (20%)
100g white maize flour (20%)
1½ tsp fine sea salt (2%)

8.00AM In a large bowl, whisk the leaven with the whey (or water and yoghurt mixture). Add the Italian "00" flour, wholewheat flour, maize flour, and salt, and stir together with your hands until you have a soft, sticky mass. The dough temperature should be about 21°C. Scrape any remaining dough from your hands, cover, and leave for 10 minutes.

8.10AM Remove the dough from the bowl and place on a lightly oiled (with corn or olive oil) or flour-dusted work-surface. Knead the dough for 10–15 seconds. Clean and dry the bowl, give it a light rub inside with oil or butter, return the dough to the bowl and leave for 10 minutes.

8.20AM Knead the dough for 10–15 seconds, shape into a ball, and then place the dough back in the bowl. Cover and leave at room temperature (around 20°C) for a further 10 minutes.

8.30AM Knead the dough for 10–15 seconds, shape into a ball, and then place the dough back in the bowl. Cover and leave for 30 minutes.

9.00AM Knead the dough for 10–15 seconds, shape into a ball, and then place the dough back in the bowl. Cover and leave for 1 hour.

10.00AM Knead the dough for 10–15 seconds, shape into a ball, and then place the dough back in the bowl. Cover and leave for 1 hour.

11.00AM Divide the dough into two pieces, each roughly 500g in weight. Shape each piece into a ball, cover, and leave on the work-surface for 15 minutes. Prepare two tea-towels, rubbing them with flour, then lay them on a tray.

11.15AM Shape the dough into long sticks (see page 21), and then place each seam-side-up on the flour-dusted cloth (or linen-lined baskets). Cover the upper surface with another cloth, and leave at room temperature (20°C) until almost doubled in height – about 2–2½ hours, as the whey hastens the speed the dough matures at.

1.30PM Preheat the oven to 220°C/425°F/gas mark 7. Dust an oven tray, or a peel if you are using an oven stone, with semolina and upturn the sticks on to this. Using a sharp blade, cut along the length of the sticks. Spray with water and bake for 50–60 minutes. Cool on a wire rack.

Barley and rye bread

Both barley and rye lack the stretchy gluten needed to hold the shape of a bold, jaunty loaf. But use them with strong white wheat flour, and let them serve submissively as a background flavour, sour with rye and dusty with barley, and you have the perfect, friendly bread.

TIP To enhance the nutty flavour of the barley flour, toast it lightly in a 180°C/350°F/gas mark 4 oven for 15 minutes, then cool before using. Simmered and soaked grains of rye and barley, well drained, can also be added to the mix.

250g rye leaven at 20°C (50%)

300g water at 20°C (60%)

300g strong white flour (60%)

100g rye flour (20%)

100g barley flour (20%)

1½ tsp fine sea salt (2%)

To make the rye leaven, see pages 25–27 and 31.

8.00AM In a large bowl, whisk the rye leaven with the water. Next, mix in the strong white flour, rye flour, barley flour and salt, and stir together with your hands until you have a soft, sticky mass. The dough temperature should be about 21°C. Scrape any remaining dough from your hands, cover, and leave for 10 minutes.

8.10AM Remove the dough from the bowl and place on a lightly oiled (with corn or olive oil) or flour-dusted work-surface. Knead the dough for 10–15 seconds. Clean and dry the bowl, give it a light rub inside with oil or butter, return the dough to the bowl and leave for 10 minutes.

8.20AM Knead the dough for 10–15 seconds, shape into a ball, and then place the dough back in the bowl. Cover and leave at room temperature (around 20°C) for a further 10 minutes.

8.30AM Knead the dough for 10–15 seconds, shape into a ball, and then place the dough back in the bowl. Cover and leave for 30 minutes.

9.00AM Knead the dough for 10–15 seconds, shape into a ball, and then place the dough back in the bowl. Cover and leave for 1 hour.

10.00AM Knead the dough for 10–15 seconds, shape into a ball, and then place the dough back in the bowl. Cover and leave for 1 hour.

11.00AM Divide the dough into two pieces, each roughly 500g in weight. Shape each piece into a ball, cover, and leave for 15 minutes. Prepare two tea-towels, rubbing them with flour, then using them to line two bowls (20cm wide), or use flour-dusted, linen-lined baskets.

11.15AM Shape the dough into balls, then place each seam-side-up on the flour-dusted cloth (or linen-lined baskets). Cover the upper surface with another cloth, and leave at room temperature (20°C) until almost doubled in height – about 5 hours.

4.30PM Preheat the oven to 220°C/425°F/gas mark 7. Dust an oven tray, or a peel if you are using an oven stone, with semolina and upturn a loaf on to this. Cut a square shape in the top of the loaf using a sharp blade. Spray the top of the loaf with water, and bake for 50–60 minutes. Cool on a wire rack. Bake the remaining loaf using the same method, or bake them at the same time if there is enough room in the oven.

Sprouted and malted grains

Sugars, stored as starch within a grain, are the plant's way of providing food for the seedling that will grow in the spring. It takes a simple process involving enzymes to convert these starches into a form the seedling can utilize. It was probably by chance that people first noticed that sprouted grains tasted sweeter when lightly roasted in a dry oven. This process of sprouting and roasting is called malting.

Many grains can be malted: wheat, barley, rye, spelt. Most of the demand for malted grains today is from the brewing industry, as malt gives beer its rich golden colour. In bread-making, malt will overcome some of the depletion in sugar that occurs in slowly fermented breads – a depletion that causes the loaf to lack colour even after a long bake and, when sliced, to toast and brown very slowly.

Malting is a skilled craft, and for anyone using a large quantity of malt, it is best to take advantage of the malted grains available from brewer's merchants or a local maltster. Mail order is always possible, and it is easy to find a supplier through the internet. But should you want to understand the process involved, and to become accepting of malt's natural place in the palette of ingredients used in breadmaking, try making a simple malt at home, which is suited to the less demanding needs of the home baker.

Bitter hops and barm

The maltose that forms naturally in the grain is rapidly utilized by the budding yeast cells, but also by other less friendly bacteria and fungi. If an infusion made from hops is added to the mash, then its mild antiseptic properties will keep the ferment sweetly fragrant. Hops give beer its slight bitterness, and were once used by both brewers and bakers to ward off a disagreeable sourness. Bakers would use a modified beer-making process, known as a "barm", beating flour into a hot, liquid mix of hops and malt so that the starch gelatinized. This proved a perfect medium for fermentation once seeded with a little of the barm from a previous week's baking. This mixture could be kept for a week, as the bitter hops would keep the mixture sweet tasting.

Until the 20th-century, when the use of commercial yeast became commonplace, bakers struggled to make bread as cleanly flavoured and white as they could. Sourness was considered a bad thing, and papers and essays were written advising bakers on how best to avoid it. The newly available processed yeast made it possible to mix and bake dough quickly which meant that the bacteria did not have time to develop and sour the loaf. Bakers rejoiced except a few.

In Scotland, for example, the bakers weren't so taken with this new, clean-tasting bread. Comparing the two breads, one made in the old style with barm, and another with the new-fangled yeast, both bakers and customers preferred the old style. But barm-making was laborious, and the new yeast convenient. And convenience won.

Sprouting and home malting

Take 200g of clean barley, and soak it for 6 hours in cold water at 15–19°C (in my home, I get that temperature in the cupboard under the sink). Pour the barley into a sieve and leave it to drain for 4 hours, stirring it occasionally with a spoon so that it dries evenly. Steep the grain once more in cold water (at 15–19°C) for 8 hours, then pour again through a sieve and transfer on to muslin or paper towel. Cover the grains with another piece of muslin (or paper towel).

Keep at 15–19°C for 4–5 days, making sure the grains stay moist with water, but not covered. Rinse the seeds once a day in fresh cold water to keep them clean. Dry in a warm room for 12 hours, then place them in an oven at its lowest setting (somewhere between 50–70°C, check with your oven thermometer) for 2–3 hours in order to lightly colour the grains, anything from golden to chocolate. Allow to cool and store in an airtight jar.

To use, grind the required amount in a coffee grinder, and add to your flour mix.

TO HOME MALT BARLEY it needs to be soaked in cold water and then allowed to dry several times over the course of a few days.

SOAKED BARLEY DRYING on a muslin cloth or paper towel.

ONCE YOUR BARLEY IS READY TO USE grind the amount you need in a coffee grinder and add to your flour mix.

A quicker barm

250g bottle-conditioned beer or ale (500%)

50g strong white flour (100%)

4 tsp white leaven (40%) (see pages 25–27)

Heat the beer or ale to 70°C in a saucepan, then remove from the heat and quickly whisk in the flour, aiming to have as few lumps as possible. Transfer to a small bowl (that the mixture will half fill), and leave to cool. When the temperature has dropped to 20°C, stir in the leaven. Cover and leave overnight, by which time it should be fermenting. Use as you would a leaven (though reduce the water accordingly in the recipe as the barm is quite liquid).

The home mashing of malt is tricky, as it is difficult to hold the mashing liquid at the right temperature. If you are interested, then a home brewing supplier can provide you with all the ingredients needed. But there is another way. A live, bottle-conditioned ale, gently heated to 70°C, can have flour whisked into it. This is a perfect replication of the complex barm of old, and once seeded with a little of your leaven, will make excellent bread. Traditionally, the fermented barm would have been mixed with a small quantity of flour from the total amount, and when this had fermented it was incorporated into the rest of the ingredients. This reduced the bitterness from the hops and produced a whiter, cleaner tasting loaf. But I don't mind the slight bitterness, so the recipe in this book skips this intermediate stage.

Barm bread

This is the traditional wheaten bread of England. It uses the barm described opposite as the leavening agent. Simply mix this with flour, water and salt, leave to rise, and then bake in a hot oven. The loaf is very simple to make, and richly flavoured from the beer-based barm, which has a slight bitterness from the green hops, and sweetness from the malted and toasted barley.

TIP Try making the barm with different beers or ales, but always look for traditional bottle-conditioned brews. Alter the flour mix, using wholewheal, rye and barley, and try simmering wholegrains in water before giving them a soak overnight in ale or mead, then drain them thoroughly before adding to the dough.

150g barm (see opposite) (30%)
250g water at 20°C (50%)
500g strong white flour (100%)
1½ tsp fine sea salt (2%)

8.00AM In a large bowl, whisk the barm with the water. Add the strong white flour and salt, and stir together with your hands until you have a soft, sticky mass. The dough temperature should be about 21°C. Scrape any remaining dough from your hands, cover, and leave for 10 minutes.

8.10AM Remove the dough from the bowl and place on a lightly oiled or flour dusted work-surface. Knead the dough for 10–15 seconds. Clean and dry the bowl, give it a light rub inside with oil or butter, return the dough to the bowl and leave for 10 minutes.

8.20AM Knead the dough for 10–15 seconds, shape into a ball, and then place the dough back in the bowl. Cover and leave at room temperature (around 20°C) for a further 10 minutes.

8.30AM Knead the dough for 10–15 seconds, shape into a ball, and then place the dough back in the bowl. Cover and leave for 30 minutes.

9.00AM Knead the dough for 10–15 seconds, shape into a ball, and then place the dough back in the bowl. Cover and leave for 1 hour.

10.00AM Knead the dough for 10–15 seconds, shape into a ball, and then place the dough back in the bowl. Cover and leave for 1 hour.

11.00AM Knead the dough for 10–15 seconds, shape into a ball, and then place the dough back in the bowl. Cover and leave for 2 hours.

1.00PM Divide the dough into two pieces, each roughly 450g in weight. Shape each piece into a ball, cover, and leave on the work-surface for 15 minutes. Prepare two tea-towels, rubbing them with flour, then using them to line two bowls (20cm wide), or use flour-dusted, linen-lined baskets.

1.15PM Shape the dough once more into balls, then place each seam-side-up in the flour-dusted cloths (or linen-lined baskets). Cover the upper surface with another cloth, and leave at room temperature (20°C) until almost doubled in height.

5.30PM Preheat the oven to 220°C/425°F/gas mark 7. Dust an oven tray, or a peel if you are using an oven stone, with semolina and upturn one loaf on to this. Using a sharp blade, cut two slashes across the loaf in the shape of a cross. Spray the top of the loaf with water, and bake for 50–70 minutes. Cool on a wire rack. Bake the remaining loaf using the same method, or bake them at the same time if there is enough room in the oven.

Crusty potato bread

250g white leaven (50%) (see pages 25–27)	75g grated scrubbed and unpeeled potato (15%)
300g water at 20°C (60%)	500g strong white flour (100%)
25g honey (5%)	1½tsp fine sea salt (2%)

This is a strongly flavoured crusty loaf that keeps moist with the grated potato and fragrant with the hint of honey. The sourness of the leaven base combines well with the two, making this a rather fine naturally leavened loaf.

8.00AM In a large bowl, whisk the leaven with the water, honey and grated potato. Add the flour and salt, and stir together with your hands until you have a soft, sticky mass. The dough temperature should be about 21°C. Scrape any remaining dough from your hands, cover, and leave for 10 minutes.

8.10AM Remove the dough from the bowl and place on a lightly oiled (with olive oil) or flour-dusted work-surface. Knead for 10–15 seconds. Clean the bowl, give it a light rub with oil or butter, return the dough to the bowl and leave for 10 minutes.

8.20AM Knead for 10–15 seconds, shape into a ball, then place the dough back in the bowl. Cover and leave at room temperature (about 20°C) for 10 minutes.

8.30AM Knead the dough for 10–15 seconds, shape into a ball, and then place the dough back in the bowl. Cover and leave for 30 minutes.

9.00AM Knead the dough for 10–15 seconds, shape into a ball, and then place the dough back in the bowl. Cover and leave for 1 hour.

10.00AM Knead the dough for 10–15 seconds, shape into a ball, and then place the dough back in the bowl. Cover and leave for 1 hour.

11.00AM Knead the dough for 10–15 seconds, shape into a ball, and then place the dough back in the bowl. Cover and leave for 1 hour.

12.00 MIDDAY Divide the dough into two pieces, each roughly 550–600g. Shape each piece into a ball, cover, and leave for 15 minutes. Rub a tea-towel with flour, then lay it on a large tray, or use a flour-dusted, linen-lined basket.

12.15PM Sit a ball of dough seam-side-upwards on the floured work-surface (see page 20). Pat it flat with your hands, then take the left and right sides furthest from you, and fold them towards the centre by 2cm, making a triangular point. Take that point and fold it inwards to the centre, pressing it down to seal. Rotate the dough 180°, then repeat with the other side. Rotate the dough, back to the start position. If you are right-handed, fold the dough in half toward you starting at the right-hand end, sealing the dough with the heel of your right hand while holding and folding it with your left. Roll the shaped loaf with both hands around it, pressing slightly more with the heel of each hand to give the ends a point. Place the dough seam-side-up on the cloth. Fold and pull the cloth up the sides of the loaf (if using a linen-lined basket, just place the dough seam-side-up inside). Repeat with the remaining dough and sit this next to the first, separated by the cloth. Cover with a cloth, and leave at room temperature (20°C) until almost doubled in height – about 4½–5 hours.

5.00–5.30PM Preheat the oven to 220°C/425°F/gas mark 7. Dust an oven tray, or peel if you're using an oven stone, with semolina. Upturn one loaf on to the tray, and make a cut along the loaf's length. Spray the top of the loaf with water, and bake for 50–70 minutes. Cool on a wire rack. Bake the remaining loaf using the same technique.

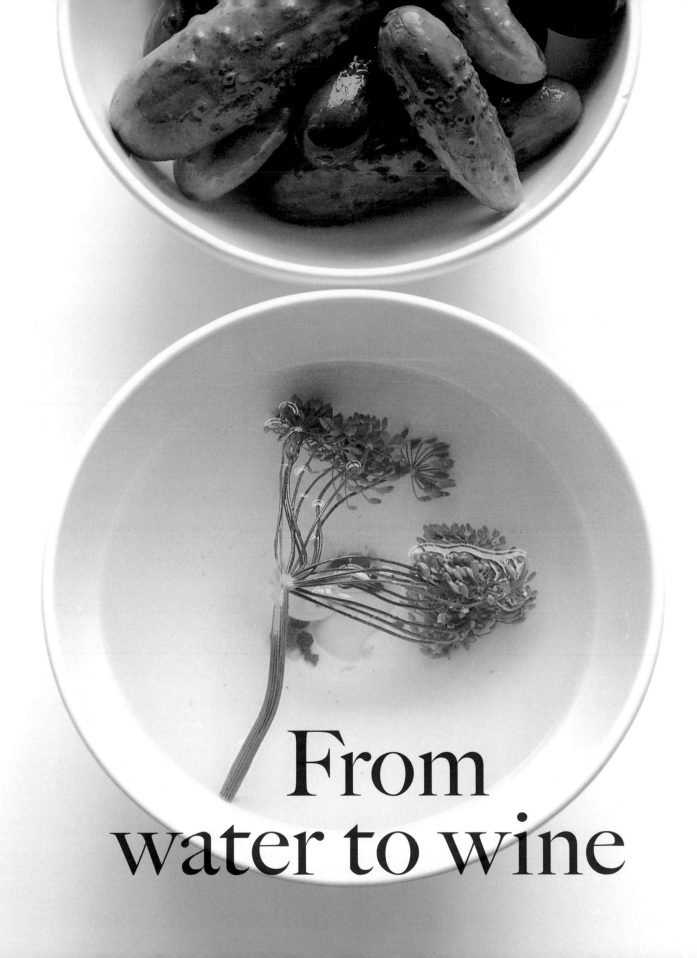

From water to wine

If you have any sense of economy, you will find that wasting food is painful. At times we all have more than we want of some things – more sun or more rain – and not every surplus can be turned to benefit. But we can be considered in our approach to meagre or lavish resources, using them respectfully and carefully.

If there is a little wine or beer left over after a bottle is opened and cooked grains remaining from a meal – a spoonful of lentils, some scrapings of rice – they can sit together in a bowl so that their flavours combine. Left overnight, these grains will plump up into juicy seeds that will moisten and hearten a whole-grain loaf. Make use of apples from a tree that is old and productive; they will need harvesting, and their flesh and sweet juice can be used in foods if we are to make the best from the crop.

On a farm, the importance of economy is more apparent. When milk is fresh and warm from the cow, it will separate into thick cream and light milk. If that milk sours, the heavy curds can be collected and salted to make cheese. The remaining opalescent liquid, called whey, can be used to create a simple loaf. No part need be wasted, discarded or poured down the drain.

It can happen in reverse. My mother would sometimes open wine when cooking the evening meal in order to add a dash to a sauce or a braise. A flagon of simple scrumpy or cider can both be used in making bread in the morning, and to drink a salute to the loaf after baking.

Water is not the only liquid we can, or should, use in bread-making. If I have water, then I will use water. But if I have other good things that need using up, then I will make the best use of them every time.

Whey bread
with butter and honey

Where to get whey? If you stir a little rennet into warm milk, the resulting curds can be strained through layers of muslin to make a simple soft cheese. The watery liquid drained off is called whey, and has traditionally been used as a liquid to make bread with. It can be either sweet or sour, depending on the condition of the milk it was strained from. It can be left over from cheese- or butter-making, or after straining yoghurt.

TIP Fromage frais, a fresh soft cheese, can be whisked into cold milk (150g cheese to 500g milk) and left overnight to sour. The following day, gently warm the sour milk so that curds form. Strain the milk through a cloth for a few hours, then lightly salt the remaining curd in the cloth (½ tsp fine sea salt for every 500g curd).

FOR THE SOFT CHEESE AND WHEY:

750g milk

1 tsp rennet

FOR THE DOUGH:

1½ tsp fresh yeast, crumbled (2%)

300g whey (60%)

50g honey (10%)

500g strong white flour (100%)

1¼ tsp fine sea salt (2%)

50g softened butter (10%)

FOR THE WHEY: Warm the milk to blood temperature (38°C). Remove from the heat. Transfer to a glass bowl and stir in the rennet quickly and evenly. Leave undisturbed in a warm place for 1 hour, so the milk solidifies into a large curd. If you gently shake the bowl, the contents should shimmer rather than cause waves. This is the old-fashioned English dessert "junket". Using a butter knife, cut the curds into small pieces. Tip both curds and whey into a colander or sieve lined with muslin set over a bowl. Refrigerate.

The following day, either lightly salt the strained curds, or leave them unsalted and sweet. Stir the curds together, and pack into a bowl lined with more muslin. You can spread nuggets of this soft cheese on a crisp cracker or on a soft slice cut from a freshly baked loaf. With the remaining whey, make a loaf of bread.

FOR THE DOUGH: In a bowl whisk the yeast with the whey and honey. Stir in 250g flour and the salt, and leave in a warm place for 30 minutes, to make a yeast batter.

Meanwhile, rub the butter into the remaining 250g flour, until it is evenly incorporated and the mixture resembles fine breadcrumbs. Stir in the yeast batter after its 30 minute rest, and mix together until you have a soft dough. Scrape any remaining dough from your hands, cover the bowl and leave for 10 minutes. Rub 1 tsp of corn or olive oil on the work-surface and knead the dough for 10 seconds, ending with the dough in a smooth, round ball. Wipe the bowl clean and rub with 1 tsp olive oil, return the dough to it, cover and leave for 10 minutes. Repeat this light kneading twice more, at 10 minute intervals, then leave the dough for 30 minutes.

At this stage the dough should be soft and elastic, with air bubbles starting to show as blisters on the outer surface. A quick small cut through the surface of the dough should show a network of air bubbles created by the yeast. Shape the dough into a ball (see page 21), and place it smooth-side down into a flour-dusted cloth. Leave in a cool place (20–24°C) for 1 hour.

Preheat the oven to 220°C/425°F/gas mark 7. Upturn the dough on to a flour-dusted baking tray, then gently spray the outside of the dough with water. Place the tray in the centre of the oven and bake for 50 minutes, or until the loaf is a good brown colour and light in weight. Cool on a wire rack.

Simple milk loaf

Soft and good for a sandwich, this milk bread contains sugars that also make it perfect for toasting. Much like the pain de mie from France, the English milk loaf has a homely appearance. But unlike t× controlled look and delicate structure of the Gallic loaf, this bread relies on the thrust created by glutinous strong white flour to jump boldly over the top of the tin. Its strong, slightly tough crumb will make a jam sandwich that can withstand the rigours of a child's schoolbag, or a cheese sandwich that can survive in a jogger's backpack.

1½ tsp fresh yeast, crumbled (2%)

350g whole milk at 20°C (70%)

20g golden or maple syrup (4%)

250g plain white flour (50%)

250g strong white flour (50%)

1¼ tsp fine sea salt (2%)

25g warm melted unsalted butter (5%)

In a large bowl, whisk the yeast with the milk and syrup. Add the flours and the salt, and squidge the lot together with your hands until you have a soft, sticky dough and the flour and liquid have evenly combined. Pour over the warm melted butter, and then squeeze this into the dough. Scrape any remaining dough from your hands, cover the bowl and leave for 10 minutes. Rub 1 tsp of olive or corn oil on the work-surface and knead the dough for 10 seconds, ending with the dough in a smooth round ball. Wipe the bowl clean and rub with 1 tsp olive oil, return the dough to it, cover and leave for a further 10 minutes. Repeat this light kneading twice more, at 10 minute intervals, then leave the dough for 30 minutes.

Grease and flour a deep loaf tin (12 x 19cm). Divide the dough into two equal pieces and shape each into a ball. Drop them side-by-side into the prepared tin, cover with a cloth, and leave to rise for 1½ hours, or until almost doubled in height.

Preheat the oven to 210°C/410°F/gas mark 6½. Brush the top of the loaf with a little cream or milk, and bake for 15 minutes, then lower the heat to 180°C/350°F/gas mark 4 and bake for a further 25–30 minutes, or until the top of the loaf is a shiny dark brown, and the loaf has come away from the sides of the tin. Remove from the tin, and leave to cool on a wire rack.

Ale bread with wheat grains

Beermaking and breadmaking have existed side-by-side for centuries. In Italy, bakers' yeast is still referred to as lievito di birra, and the barm-making practice that lasted in Scotland well into the 20th century used a modified beer recipe, in which flour was whisked into the hot liquor left from the mashing of malted grains and the boiling of hops. These hops gave the liquor slight anti-bacterial properties, and helped keep the ferment from souring (for much of our baking history, the aim was to ferment dough rather than to sour it). Now we rely on lactic ferments to protect our food from more harmful bacteria, a form of natural preservation. But enough. The beer-soaked grains used here are simply good to eat, and their moistness helps keep the crumb sticky-soft for many days.

300g strong white flour (60%)

150g rye flour (30%)

50g strong wholewheat flour (10%)

1½ tsp fine sea salt (2%)

200g ale (40%)

100g water at 20°C (20%)

300g white leaven (60%) (see pages 25–27)

¾ tsp fresh yeast, crumbled (1%)

10g ground malted grains (2%)
  (see page 39)

200g cooked wheat grains (40%),
  (see opposite, but soaked overnight
  in ale rather than wine)

Combine the three flours, and mix with the salt. In another bowl, whisk the ale and water with the leaven and yeast, together with the ground malt and ale-soaked wheat. Then add the flour. Mix both together with your hands, squeezing it through your fingertips. When roughly combined, cover the bowl and leave it for 10 minutes. Knead gently on a lightly oiled surface for 10–15 seconds, until combined. Return the dough to the bowl, leave for a further 30 minutes, then knead once more for a further 10–15 seconds.

Give the dough a turn (see page 19), and repeat the turning after 30 minutes and 1 hour. Dust a tea-towel with rye flour, and line a 2-litre bowl with this (or use a flour-dusted proving basket). Shape the dough into a ball and place seam-side-up in the cloth. Cover and leave for 2 hours, or until doubled in size.

Preheat the oven to 210°C/410°F/gas mark 6½. Carefully upturn the dough on to a flour-dusted baking sheet, and cut a Union Jack of slashes across the upper surface. Bake in the centre of the oven for 45 minutes, until the loaf is a good rich brown in colour and, when tapped on the bottom, sounds hollow. Leave to cool on a wire rack.

Alsace loaf with rye

The crisp fruitiness of an Alsace wine provides a gentle marinade for the cooked rye grains. Sometimes these grains are called "berries", and the description makes sense when you taste them cooked in this way. The rye grains swell and soften during the initial cooking in water, and then overnight the wine plumps up each grain and adds a slightly sharp sweetness, and you can happily eat the grains by the handful. If you don't want to use alcohol, then replace this marinade with either thin yoghurt or a good cold-pressed fruit juice.

FOR THE GRAINS (makes 300g of soaked grains):

200g whole rye grains

water to cover

200g white wine

FOR THE DOUGH:

350g strong white flour (70%)

100g soft wholemeal flour (20%)

50g rye flour (10%)

325g water at 20°C (65%)

¾ tsp fresh yeast, crumbled (1%)

25g honey (5%)

150g rye leaven (30%)

 (see pages 25–27 and 31)

300g wine-soaked grains, drained (60%)

1¼ tsp fine sea salt (3%)

25g melted butter, lard or oil (5%)

FOR THE GRAINS In a small saucepan, mix the rye grains with the water. Bring the mixture to the boil, then lower the heat and simmer for 45 minutes, if necessary topping the saucepan up with extra water so that the grains are always covered by liquid. Remove from the heat, transfer the grains and remaining cooking liquid to a container and, when cool, strain (this liquid can be used in place of the water in the recipe) and cover with wine (or yoghurt or juice). Place in the refrigerator, or another cool place, overnight. Drain before use.

FOR THE DOUGH Mix the flours lightly together and leave to one side. In a second bowl, place the water, fresh yeast, and honey, stir well and leave the mixture to sit for 10 minutes. Add the leaven (broken into small pieces) and grains to the yeasted mixture. Stir this mixture into the dry ingredients, then mix together well with your hands, squeezing it through your fingertips. When roughly combined, cover the bowl and leave it for 10 minutes. Tip the dough out on to a lightly floured work-surface, sprinkle over the salt and melted butter, and knead gently for 10–15 seconds, until combined. Return the dough to the bowl, leave for a further 30 minutes, then knead once more for a further 10–15 seconds.

Give the dough a turn (see page 19), and repeat every half hour for 1½ hours (do not turn it at the end of this time). Divide the dough into five pieces, each just over 250g. Roll each piece into a stick or baton (see page 21), lay each seam-side-up on a flour-dusted cloth, and leave to rise for 1 hour.

Preheat the oven to 210°C/410°F/gas mark 6½. Carefully upturn two or three of the sticks of dough out on to a flour-dusted baking sheet, and cut three or four slashes diagonally across the upper surface. Bake in the centre of the oven for 35 minutes, until the sticks are a good rich brown colour and, when tapped on the bottom, sound hollow. Leave to cool on a wire rack and bake the remaining bread.

Ukraine

Yaroslava Kharuk, her son Andrei, and their Rottweiler, Jack, live in a 1950s block in the Ukraine city of Ivano-Frankivsk in a three-room apartment with a small kitchen annex. Jack is a bear of a dog, his coat shines and his eyes are bright. He's fed bread and gravy, or cabbage and potatoes, cooked at the same time as the evening meal. Yaroslava cooks with little waste. Scraps are fed to Jack or used in other dishes. Most of the ingredients come from her parents' farm, with soft cheese and milk from the family cow and carrots and potatoes from the fields her father has ploughed.

This morning's breakfast consists of fried farm eggs, each with a deep-yellow yolk, dark rye bread, fresh butter, coffee,

different pork cuts, sausages, and apricot juice. Then we head for the street market to buy flour, fresh yeast, and salt.

Vans are parked with their rear doors open to display trayfuls of bread, collected by each seller from the local bakeries and supplemented with loaves baked at home and by friends. There are a dozen different rye breads, each labelled with the ingredients and price. Subtle variations between ingredients in bread are noticed and appreciated by customers in Eastern Europe, whereas in the West we have moved stridently towards bolder, more obvious contrasts in taste. Appreciating slight differences requires knowledge and some understanding of the way

LEFT PAGE, CLOCKWISE FROM TOP LEFT: Sister Joanna holds open a recipe book from the convent; the chapel ceiling at the Ukrainian Greek-Catholic Church; animals and fishermen by the river Dnister; Maria in front of her wood-fired oven; loaves sold from a van at a street market in Ivano-Frankivsk THIS PAGE, CLOCKWISE FROM TOP LEFT: Mykola Kobylansky, mayor of Pidverbchi; Sister Joanna sifting flour; plaiting dough for *paska*; *talena*, a local red berry, preserved and used as a remedy; an ornate barn; dough rising; eggs being beaten; dark rye bread with a glass of vodka steeped with *talena* berries.

RIGHT: Maria uses a brush of chicken feathers;
RIGHT: Wasyl with the happy pigs in the yard.

> "If a girl married, her plait of hair would be cut and nailed to the roof of their house. Now we have a loaf." SISTER JOANNA

local history has affected each bread. The different, often symbolic, shapes of bread result in different flavours and textures, since the distance warmth must travel through the unbaked dough will affect fermentation, and the time the loaf spends in the oven will affect the flavour.

We travel near the foothills of the Carpathian Mountains to a village called Pidverbchi, where Yaroslava's parents, Maria and Wasyl, have a small farm surrounded by bare, ploughed fields where the stumps of cabbage stalks stick out like stakes from the ground. "When I was 20 and married a year," Maria tells me as she puts a flame to the wood in the oven, "I had been left to bake bread. I didn't know how much wood to use, so I packed the oven full and set it alight. There were flames everywhere, and Wasyl was terrified the house would burn down. I got a bucket of water and threw it in, and that put the fire out. Then I tried to relight it, but everything was soaking. That's how I learned that bread doesn't need much wood."

Outside the house there are two wells: one that collects rainwater and the other filled by a spring in the ground. "Rainwater is softer and better for washing," says Maria, "and well-water is better for cooking." She mixes a little whey, strained from soft cheese, with yeast and a spoonful of flour. This is left for a few hours beside the oven while I walk with Wasyl and my translator, Oxana, to the river

Dnister to pick berries and see what the fishermen have caught. Along the riverbank, cows and goats are grazing. Each family takes it in turn to walk the cattle to new pasture.

Back at the farmhouse, the yeast mixture is bubbling. Maria mixes it with flour, salt, eggs, and well-water to form a sticky dough. This is kneaded gently, then left to rise. An old oblong tin is greased lightly, then the dough is divided, shaped into a baton, tucked into the tin, and left to double in height. Finally, Maria goes to the yard and collects long chicken feathers. She ties these together with thread, uses them to brush a beaten egg on to the dough's surface and puts the tin in the oven. We eat the bread early that evening, with small fried potato cakes, pickled tomatoes, and local ham. The bread has a slightly sour tang and a creamy taste in the crumb. It is good and comforting.

Days later we visit the convent of the Sisters Meronocyts, part of the Ukrainian Greek-Catholic Church that reformed after *perestroika* in 1991, having been banned during the Soviet era. Part of the sisters' daily work is bread-baking, and this continued even during the years without a convent. Mother Theresa joined the convent when she was 15, before it was legal. "In 1952 the soldiers gave the sisters 24 hours to leave the convent and dismantle the Church. From then on we practised the faith in secret, meeting at one of the sister's homes and praying in the quiet of a bedroom. Every so often someone would be arrested and imprisoned."

This convent, built after *perestroika*, has a glazed-tile wood-oven. "We make enriched breads plaited and twisted into ceremonial shapes, typically for weddings, Easter, and Christmas. *Kolach* is an important bread," says Mother Theresa. "When someone dies it is usual to have a service at home. On the table there will be holy water, a loaf of *Kolach*, and a candle." The plait, too, is symbolic. Sister Joanna tells me: "My grandmother said that years ago, when a girl married, her plait of hair would be cut and nailed to the roof of their house. Now we have a loaf, and everyone is happier."

LEFT TO RIGHT: Svetlana, Jergenia and Avanna stock the shelves with bread at a bakery in Bogorogchany; baker Vitaliy holding a stack of light rye bread.

Scrumpy buns

In *The Book of Apples* Joan Morgan describes how during the Middle Ages "cider and ale battled for first place in the English tankard". Such was the popularity of cider, yet it now lags behind. The fermented juice of apples could either be brewed to a standard comparable to fine wine, or left coarse and lowly as simple scrumpy. These large buns use the latter combined with barley and malt, giving the crumb a caramel tint and smoky flavour.

TIP You can stir 1 tsp of the leaven with sweet unpasteurised apple juice, leave it overnight, and use the subsequent fermented liquor in place of water in your bread-making.

300g strong white flour (60%)

200g barley flour (40%)

10g home malted barley, ground (2%)
(see page 39)

1½ tsp fine sea salt (2%)

325g scrumpy or cider (65%)

200g white leaven (40%)
(see pages 25–27)

1¼ tsp fresh yeast, crumbled (1%)

extra cider for brushing the loaves

flakes of sea salt to sprinkle on top

Combine the flours with the ground malted barley, and mix with the salt. In another bowl, whisk the scrumpy or cider with the leaven and yeast. Mix this liquid together with the dry ingredients using your hands, squeezing it through your fingertips. When roughly combined, cover the bowl and leave for 10 minutes. Tip the dough out on to a lightly floured work-surface, and knead gently for 10–15 seconds, until combined. Return the dough to the bowl, leave for a further 30 minutes, then knead once more for 10–15 seconds.

Give the dough a turn (see page 19), and repeat after 30 minutes and 1 hour. Divide the dough into five pieces, each weighing roughly 200g. Round each piece into a ball and sit them on a baking tray, evenly spaced (i.e. one towards each corner and one in the middle). Cover with a cloth and leave to rise for 2 hours, or until nearly doubled in height.

Preheat the oven to 210°C/410°F/gas mark 6½. Brush the top of each bun with scrumpy (or cider) and sprinkle with salt flakes. Bake in the centre of the oven for 35 minutes, until the buns are a good rich brown colour and, when tapped on the bottom, sound hollow. Leave to cool on a wire rack.

Red wine loaf with pine nuts and figs

This loaf is a hybrid, and was inspired by two bakers – one I still know, and one I only have a memory of. I worked at Baker & Spice with a young Frenchman, who told me about a long walnut baton that he made by storing the nuts in good red wine, and using both the ruddied nuts and the dark wine in the loaf. The other baker, Federico Turi, made a round, crusty fig and raisin bread at Locanda Locatelli, but the mixing caused the fruit pieces to disappear, with only the flecks of tiny seeds remaining. Here, the two loaves become one in a flat disc that gives maximum crust, the crumb studded with ruby-coated pine nuts and with a crunch on the teeth from fig seeds.

FOR THE NUTS AND FIGS (makes 350g when soaked and strained):

250g red wine

100g pine nuts

200g dried figs, cut into eighths

FOR THE DOUGH:

250g strong white flour (50%)

250g strong wholewheat flour (50%)

1½ tsp fine sea salt (2%)

260g reserved wine from soaking, made up with water (52%)

1¼ tsp fresh yeast, crumbled (1%)

150g white leaven (30%) (see pages 25–27)

350g nuts and figs, strained (70%)

FOR THE NUTS AND FIGS In a saucepan, place the wine, pine nuts, and chopped figs. Bring to the boil, then simmer for a minute. Remove from the heat and leave covered overnight, stirring the mixture once before you go to bed. Next day, strain the liquid off, reserving it and making it up to 260g with water.

FOR THE DOUGH Combine the flours, and mix with the salt. In another bowl, whisk the water (and wine) with the leaven and yeast, together with the pine nuts and figs. Mix the flour and liquid together with your hands, squeezing it through your fingertips. When roughly combined, cover the bowl and leave it for 10 minutes. Tip the dough out on to a lightly floured work-surface, and knead gently for 10–15 seconds, until combined. Return the dough to the bowl, leave for a further 30 minutes then knead once more for 10–15 seconds.

Give the dough a turn (see page 19), and repeat after 30 minutes and 1 hour. Dust a tea-towel with rye flour and lay this over a tray. Divide the dough into two equal pieces and, using a little flour to dust the work-surface, knead each into a ball. Leave to sit, covered, on the work-surface for 5 minutes, so that the dough has a chance to soften after kneading. Next, using flour to stop the dough from sticking, roll each piece of dough out into a flat oval shape 2cm thick. Place these side-by-side on the floured cloth, and cover with another cloth. Leave to rise for 1½ hours.

Preheat the oven to 210°C/410°F/gas mark 6½. Brush oil over the upper surface of the dough, then cut criss-cross slashes across the upper surface with a sharp knife or blade. Carefully transfer the dough to a flour-dusted baking sheet, and bake in the centre of the oven for 45 minutes, until the loaf is a good rich brown colour and, when tapped on the bottom, sounds hollow. Leave to cool on a wire rack.

Cucumber pickle juice rye loaf

This is a simple sour rye in which all of the souring comes from the cucumber pickle juice. It's a very good hearty bread, made darker by the toasted rye flour that colours the crumb without the need for malt or treacle. Cucumber pickle juice is simply the slightly salty, slightly vinegary juice in a jar of pickled cucumbers. Either eat the pickles before using the left-over juice or drain off the juice and replace it with water, with a little salt and vinegar added.

TIP To get the polished oak crust in the picture, make a starch paste by using 20g rye flour mixed with 150g cold water, and whisk as you heat this to boiling point. Then allow the paste to cool, thinning it with water until it is the consistency of thin pouring cream. 15 minutes before the end of baking, remove the loaf from the oven and quickly brush this over the uncut surface. Put the loaf back in the oven and finish the baking.

200g toasted rye flour (40%) (see below)

300g strong white flour (60%)

¾ tsp fine sea salt (1%)

350g cucumber pickle juice at 20°C (70%)

1¼ tsp fresh yeast, crumbled (1%)

10g (2 good sprigs) fresh dill, chopped (2%)

To toast the rye flour, preheat the oven to 200°C/400°F/gas mark 6. Spread the rye flour in a thin layer over a baking sheet, and bake for 15 minutes, or until the flour has turned a light tannish brown. Remove from the oven and allow to cool.

Combine the flours, and mix with the salt. In another bowl, whisk the pickle juice with yeast and dill. Mix this liquid and the flour together with your hands, squeezing it through your fingertips. When roughly combined, cover the bowl and leave it for 10 minutes. Tip the dough out on to a lightly oiled (with corn or olive oil) work-surface and knead gently for 10–15 seconds. Return the dough to the bowl, leave for a further 10 minutes, then knead once more for 10–15 seconds. Return the dough to the bowl, leave for 10 minutes again, then knead one final time for 10–15 seconds.

Give the dough a turn (see page 19), and repeat after 30 minutes and 1 hour. Divide the dough into two equal pieces, and shape each into a round. Place both on a flour-dusted baking sheet, leaving a space between for the loaves to grow. Cover and leave for 1 hour, or until doubled in size.

Preheat the oven to 210°C/410°F/gas mark 6½. Cut a slash across the centre of each loaf. Bake in the centre of the oven for 55 minutes, until the loaves are a good rich brown colour and, when tapped on the bottom, sound hollow. Leave to cool on a wire rack.

Sweet brandy buns

The British were a nation of bun eaters, but then innuendo got the better of us. Now we are happier nibbling the nipple off a *brioche à tête*. There were once great bun shops, selling the famous buns of Chelsea, Albion (with buttermilk and eggs), Exeter (with butter and eggs), Dublin (twisted with caraway and currants), and Bath (with peel and sultanas). This is my stand to resurrect the grand tradition of the bun. Eat them with the best jam and the softest cream.

TIP Just before baking, the buns are brushed with more brandy and dredged with caster sugar but you could use any spirit that you have to douse the top. The Catalan *coca di forno* is brushed with anise spirit before being sprinkled with sugar and pine nuts prior to baking.

FOR THE FERMENT:

125g whole milk (83%)

1½ tsp fresh yeast, crumbled (2%)

50g caster sugar (33%)

150g strong white flour (100%)

50g double cream (33%)

FOR THE DOUGH:

350g strong white flour (100%)

1½ tsp tsp fine sea salt (3%)

100g butter, softened (28%)

1 medium egg (14%)

50g brandy (14%)

the ferment (110%)

extra brandy for brushing the buns

extra caster sugar for dredging the buns

FOR THE FERMENT Whisk all of the ingredients together in a large bowl, cover, and leave in a warm place (20–22°C) for 30 minutes.

FOR THE DOUGH In a bowl, mix the flour and salt together, then rub the softened butter into it until there are no lumps and the flour starts to resemble fine breadcrumbs. Whisk the egg and brandy into the ferment, then work the mixture into the buttered flour, squeezing it through your fingertips. When roughly combined, cover the bowl and leave it for 10 minutes. Tip the dough out on to a lightly oiled work-surface and knead gently for 10–15 seconds. Return the dough to the bowl, leave for a further 10 minutes, then knead once more for a further 10–15 seconds. Return the dough to the bowl, leave for a further 10 minutes then knead one final time for 10–15 seconds.

Give the dough a turn (see page 19), and repeat after 30 minutes and 1 hour. Line two baking trays with non-stick baking parchment (or use well-buttered brown paper). Divide the dough into 12 pieces, each weighing roughly 80g. Round each into a bun and sit them seam-side-down on the baking sheets, evenly spaced. Cover with a dry cloth and leave to rise in a cool place (15–18°C) for 1½–2 hours.

Preheat the oven to 200°C/400°F/gas mark 6. Brush the surface of the buns with the extra brandy, then dredge them lightly with the additional caster sugar. Bake in the centre of the oven for 15 minutes, then reduce the heat to 180°C/350°F/gas mark 4 and bake for a further 10–15 minutes, until the buns are golden brown. Leave to cool on a wire rack. When cold, place in a paper bag (or freeze) to help them stay soft.

Cassis and currant loaf

FOR THE SOAKED CURRANTS (makes 280g when soaked and strained):

250g currants

150g water

50g cassis

FOR THE DOUGH:

250g strong white flour (50%)

100g strong wholewheat flour (20%)

150g rye flour (30%)

1½ tsp fine sea salt (2%)

280g soaked currants, drained (56%)

150g soaking liquid plus water to make the required weight at 20°C (30%)

30g cassis at 20°C (6%)

100g water at 20°C (20%)

¾ tsp fresh yeast, crumbled (1½%)

200g rye leaven (40%) (see pages 25–27 and 31)

Currants are tiny dried black grapes, whereas blackcurrants are little dark fruits from a relative of the gooseberry. But when combined in this way, their flavours unite and form a single, intense "currant" taste. For this bread, the currants are simmered gently in water and cassis, then the mixture is left overnight. The following day, the strained liquid adds sweetness and colour to the loaf, while the plump currants stud the crumb. Rye and blackcurrants are good partners, and the loaf can be made well with dried blackcurrants. The currants and rye can also be partnered with dark red grape juice.

TIP If you have a large crop of blackcurrants, they can be home-dried by spreading them out on a sheet of wire gauze (stretched over a square wooden frame), and left in the sun to bake until shrivelled – but not as hard as stones. Alternatively, pack them in a jar, layered with caster sugar and then covered with vodka or *eau de vie*.

FOR THE SOAKED CURRANTS Rinse the currants, then place in a saucepan and cover with the water and cassis. Bring to the boil, then remove from the heat and leave to cool overnight.

FOR THE DOUGH Combine the flours, and mix with the salt. In another bowl, whisk the soaked currants with the measured soaking liquid and water, extra cassis, water, yeast, and rye leaven.

Mix this liquid with the flour and salt, squeezing it through your fingertips. When evenly combined, cover the bowl and leave it for 10 minutes. Tip the dough out on to a lightly oiled (with corn or olive oil) work-surface and knead gently for 10–15 seconds. Return the dough to the bowl, leave for a further 10 minutes, then knead once more for a further 10–15 seconds. Return the dough to the bowl, leave for a further 10 minutes, then knead one final time for 10–15 seconds.

Give the dough a turn (see page 19), and repeat after 30, 60, and 90 minutes. Dust two tea-towels with rye flour, and line two oblong loaf tins (20 x 10cm) with these. They will act as the proving baskets (or use flour-dusted cane proving baskets if you have them). Shape the dough into a baton (see page 21) and place each loaf seam-side-up in the cloth. Cover and leave for 2 hours, or until doubled in size. At this point, I have left the loaf overnight in the refrigerator, and it bakes perfectly the next morning.

Preheat the oven to 210°C/410°F/gas mark 6½. Carefully upturn one loaf on to a flour-dusted baking sheet, and cut a single slash down the centre of the upper surface. Brush or spray water along the cut, and bake in the centre of the oven for 45 minutes, until the loaf is a good rich brown colour and, when tapped on the bottom, sounds hollow. Leave to cool on a wire rack. Then bake the other loaf, or put them both in the oven at the same time if there is room.

From
field to mill

It starts with a grain. A single grain, perhaps an heirloom, is planted, harvested, and the seeds collected to be planted again, either in the late autumn or the following spring, depending on the variety. It will be harvested the following summer. Once again, those seeds are collected, planted, and harvested. That single stem of wheat has now been replaced by a patch of wheat, and that single grain has become a small bag of grain. And so, once more, the new crop of seeds is planted, fed by the rain, the nutrients in the soil, and the sunlight. To be harvested and scattered into the soil once more.

Of course you could easily go to a seed merchant and buy a sack of prepared, nutrient-washed, and genetically-sturdy grain. These are the popular plants, the ones that are fashionable and trouble-free, and the ones that make money for their seller. The other grains, though, need to find a less grasping champion.

The plants that cover the land are as important to the heritage of a country as its books, music, and customs. Many have disappeared, some only remain as photographs or drawings, but a few lucky specimens lie tucked away and secure in national archives for plants and seeds. If an enterprising farmer wants to replant a local variety that has long disappeared, it is to these archives he or she must go. Sometimes seeds have travelled far, and hidden in another country's archive might be an immigrant that, through good fortune, might be replanted once more back home.

Quick white loaf

This is a close-textured, soft white bread, with no pretence to be anything other than that. Make a sandwich with a peppery, in-season tomato, sea salt, and a little sweet butter. When I was a child at the beach, my aunt would make sandwiches with such a loaf, filled with garden-fresh lettuce leaves, butter and the inevitable crunch of stray sand.

TIP The small amount of milk in this recipe helps the bread to colour, and the decent amount of yeast will ensure that as the loaf rises quickly it won't lose any of the natural sugars in the wheat flour, which means that a slice of bread will toast nicely. There is a fleck of millet throughout the dough, giving the crumb a slightly creamy colour.

Clean the bowl as the dough sits on the work-surface after the first knead. This applies equally to all of the breads, as it helps keep the dough free of stray hard lumps that might flake off a dirty bowl.

200g whole milk at 20°C (40%)

150g water at 20°C (30%)

2 tsp fresh yeast, crumbled (2%)

200g plain white flour (40%)

300g strong white flour (60%)

optional: 50g millet flakes (10%)

1½ tsp fine sea salt (2%)

Mix the milk and water together. Crumble the yeast into the liquid and whisk it gently until dissolved. Combine the dry ingredients, then mix with the liquid until you have a sticky but cohesive mass. Cover the bowl with a cloth and leave for 10 minutes.

Rub 1 tsp of corn or olive oil on the work-surface and knead the dough for 10 seconds, ending with the dough in a smooth, round ball.

Clean and dry the bowl, then rub lightly with a tsp of oil. Return the dough to the bowl, cover, and leave for a further 10 minutes.

Remove the dough and knead once more on the oiled surface, returning the shape to a smooth, round ball. Place it back in the bowl, cover, and leave for 1¼ hours in a warmish (21–25°C) place.

Divide the dough into two pieces, each weighing just over 400g. Shape each into a ball on a lightly floured surface and leave covered for 5 minutes.

Lay a flat dinner tray with a tea-towel (or use oblong baskets if you have them), and dredge heavily with flour, rubbing it into the cloth so that it is evenly spread.

Sit one ball of dough seam-side-upwards on the floured work-surface. To shape the dough (see page 20), pat it flat with your hands into an oval 15cm front-to-back and slightly longer left-to-right. Take the left and right sides furthest from you and fold them inwards towards the centre by 2cm, making a triangular point. Next, take that same point and fold it inwards to the centre, pressing it firmly down to seal. Rotate the dough 180°, and repeat with the other side. Rotate the dough once more, so that you are back in the starting position.

If you are right-handed, fold the dough in half towards you starting at the right-hand end, sealing the dough with the heel of your right hand while holding and folding the dough with your left. Roll the shaped loaf (with both hands tucked around it) on the work-surface, pressing down slightly more with the heel of each hand to give the ends a gentle point. Lift the dough and place it seam-side-upwards on the cloth. Finally, fold and pull the cloth up the sides of the loaf (or if using a flour-dusted basket, simply place the seam-side upwards inside). Leave to rise for 1½ hours, or until almost doubled in height.

Preheat the oven to 220°C/425°F/gas mark 7. Turn the dough on to a flour-dusted baking sheet. Using a sharp knife, cut two or three slashes in the upper surface of each. Bake for at least 45 minutes, or until each loaf is a good golden brown.

Wheatgerm bread

Early in the 20th-century doctors became increasingly aware that the health of the population was built on diet. Fibre, from the grain's outer husk, has essential benefits to our digestion; it is how our body extracts the nutrients it needs to survive and grow. Should this process struggle, then our health is compromised. In this recipe, the combination of wheatgerm, wholewheat flour, and wholewheat grains, gives you as much flavour and fibre as you could wish for in a loaf, plus a rich, natural caramel colour.

TIP In an act of breadmaking heresy, this bread doesn't really have an initial fermentation. After kneading, the dough is left for 10 minutes before being shaped and placed in the tin, so most of the fermentation occurs once the dough is in its final shape.

Breadmaking flour has a lot of strong gluten, but it is contained within the endosperm. In white flour, all that remains is the milled endosperm; in wholewheat flour this is a smaller percentage of the dry matter. Wholewheat flours should therefore be treated as if they contain less gluten, which means you need to handle the dough less and give it a shorter initial rise. This bread has an extra 25 per cent wheatgerm, which lowers the gluten content further. Be gentle with the kneading, as the bran will tear the gluten if the dough is subjected to a rigorous and extended mixing.

40g wholewheat grains, plus water to cover (10%)

100g wheatgerm (25%)

400g strong wholewheat flour (100%)

¾ tsp fine sea salt (1%)

340g water at 20°C (85%)

60g orange juice at 20°C (15%)

40g honey (10%)

1¾ tsp fresh yeast, crumbled (2.5%)

Place the wholewheat grains in a small saucepan, cover with water and simmer for 30 minutes, ensuring they remain covered with water at all times. Remove from the heat, add cold water to the pan so that the grains become lukewarm, then drain. Preheat the oven to 180°C/350°F/gas mark 4.

Pour the wheatgerm on to a clean baking sheet, and bake for 12 minutes, shaking or stirring the tray halfway through to ensure that the germ toasts rather than burns or stays pale. Leave to cool or, if your flour is particularly cold (if the kitchen is freezing one morning, for example), tip the hot wheatgerm into the flour and toss it through your fingers.

Put the flour, salt, and toasted wheatgerm in a large mixing bowl. In another bowl or jug, mix the measured water, orange juice, and honey, and stir in the crumbled yeast and the cooked wholewheat grains. When the yeast has dissolved, add the liquid to the dry ingredients and mix with your hands. When evenly combined, cover the bowl with a cloth and leave for 5 minutes.

Meanwhile, grease and flour a deep, narrow 9 x 24cm loaf tin. Rub 1 tsp of corn or olive oil on to the work-surface. Remove the dough from the bowl and knead for 10 seconds. Shape the dough back into a ball, then return it to the bowl and leave for 5 minutes. Repeat the short kneading, shape into a ball once more, return to the bowl and leave for another 5 minutes. Knead the dough one final time, shape into a ball once more, and leave for 10 minutes.

Pat the dough into a flat rectangle measuring roughly 25cm left-to-right x 20cm front-to-back. Roll the dough inward, starting at the end furthest from you, rolling it tightly as you do. Roll the dough gently on the work-surface, then tap the ends inward so that it will drop neatly into the prepared tin.

Cover the tin with a cloth and leave to rise in a warm (21–25°C) place for 1½ hours, or until it has risen about 1cm over the top of the tin. Using a sharp blade, make several diagonal slashes across the surface of the loaf.

Preheat the oven to 220°C/425°F/gas mark 7. Place the tin in the centre of the oven and bake for a minimum of 45 minutes, or until the top of the loaf is a golden brown colour, and the sides of the loaf have pulled away from the tin. Remove from the oven, leave for 5 minutes, then remove from the tin and leave to cool on a wire rack. When cold, wrap in waxed paper and either freeze or eat over the following few days.

Sweet rye bread

FOR THE OVERNIGHT BATTER: (makes 290g)

240g boiling water

50g fine rye flour

OPTIONAL SPICES:

seeds from 3 cardamom pods, crushed

1 tsp aniseed

zest of 1 orange

FOR THE DOUGH:

200g rye leaven (67%)
   (see pages 25–27 and 31)

140g honey (47%)

50g water at 20°C (17%)

290g overnight batter (97%) (see above)

300g fine rye flour (100%)

1 tsp fine sea salt (2%)

FOR THE OVERNIGHT BATTER Cool the water until it reads 80°C on a thermometer. Slowly whisk in the rye flour, ensuring that the mixture is free of lumps. Cover and leave overnight.

FOR THE DOUGH Beat the rye leaven, honey, and water together with the overnight batter. Add the remaining rye flour and salt. Stir until you have a thick, evenly mixed paste. As there is no elastic gluten in the rye flour, the gluten it does contain is sticky and does not require kneading. If you are using the additional spices and flavours, then add them now.

Oil and flour a 17cm square tin. Scrape the dough from the bowl into the tin and smooth the top with a spatula. Cover with a cloth and leave in a warm (25°C) place for 5–6 hours, or until doubled in height.

Preheat the oven to 200°C/400°F/gas mark 6. Oil a sheet of foil and wrap it snugly over the top of the baking tin. Bake for 1½ hours, then carefully remove the foil from the top and bake for a further 1 hour, so that the upper crust darkens. In Sweden this loaf would traditionally have a charred black crust on top. Leave to cool in the tin. When cold, remove from the tin and wrap well in oiled paper. Leave for two days before eating, as this will make slicing easier.

I wonder if it is the steel grey colour that makes us reluctant to embrace rye flour? Across northern Europe, rye is the one bread that is found everywhere, from the motorway truck-stop café to the bread bin in the hillside farmhouse. But here in Britain and the US, it is only in the finer restaurants and shops that rye bread is celebrated; what was once the bread of the poor has become the staple of the rich man's table.

TIP The bread's natural tang can be calmed by a shaving of unsalted butter, and together they form a perfect pairing to accompany those other runaway paupers, fresh oysters and smoked eel.

OPPOSITE PAGE, FROM TOP LEFT:
1 Above, rye leaven; below, overnight batter.
2 The mixed dough.
3 The dough scraped into the tin.
4 The risen dough.

1 2
3 4

Light caraway rye bread

FOR THE FERMENT:

125g water at 20°C (71%)

50g sour milk (see tip) (28%)

1 tsp fresh yeast, crumbled (3%)

175g rye flour (100%)

FOR THE DOUGH:

1 tsp caraway seeds (1%)

50g rye flour (25%)

150g strong white flour (75%)

1 tsp fine sea salt (2%)

125g water at 20°C (62%)

¼ tsp fresh yeast, crumbled (0.5%)

1 tsp malt (2.5%)

1 tbsp melted butter (7%)

The ferment (175%)

This bread is similar to those found in the markets in Lviv, in the western Ukraine. I wrote this recipe while baking with the Sisters Meronocyts, at their convent in Ivano-Frankivsk, and it is a faithful reflection of that rye bread. It uses caraway, a traditional ingredient in many rye breads. Caraway is one of the seeds from the parsley family, and was traditionally used both as a flavouring and as a medicinal aid, thought to ease chest and throat infections and to sooth digestion.

TIP The loaf uses sour milk, which I found frequently used in cooking and baking in the Ukraine. On farms, the milk collected from the cow would be poured into plastic mineral water bottles, where it would separate and sour naturally after a few days. Pasteurized milk won't sour, as it lacks the natural bacteria to do this; but a few teaspoons of yoghurt or buttermilk, or even lemon juice, stirred into the milk and left to stand for 30 minutes, will give a vague imitation of the souring process.

FOR THE FERMENT Mix together the water and sour milk, then stir in the yeast. Add the rye flour and stir until evenly combined. Cover and leave in a warm (21–25°C) place for 2 hours, until risen and the inner dough is clearly fermenting. To check this is happening, break the surface of the ferment with a spoon: you should see a network of bubbles underneath, and the mixture will have almost doubled in height.

FOR THE DOUGH Preheat the oven to 180°C/350°F/gas mark 4. On a clean baking tray, sprinkle the caraway seeds and bake for 10–12 minutes, so they warm and begin to release their fragrance.

Put the flours and salt in a large bowl. In a jug, whisk the water with the yeast, malt and most of the toasted caraway seeds, holding back a few to scatter on top of the loaf. Add the liquid to the ferment, mix lightly but evenly together, then add all this to the flour. Using your hands, mix the dough until it is soft and well combined.

Grease and flour an oblong 9 x 20cm loaf tin. On a lightly oiled (with corn or olive oil) work-surface, tap the dough out into a 10cm square, then roll up into a cylinder that will fit snugly in the tin. Drop it in, seam-side down, then squish it down with your knuckles to flatten the top. Sprinkle the remaining caraway seeds on top, cover and leave to rise for 1½ hours.

Preheat the oven to 220°C/425°F/gas mark 7. Place the loaf tin in the centre of the oven and bake for 30 minutes, then brush the top of the loaf with a little melted butter and continue to bake for a further 20 minutes, or until the loaf has pulled away from the sides of the tin and the buttered top is a dark shiny brown. Leave to cool on a wire rack. When cool, wrap in waxed paper.

Waterford soda bread

300g soft wholewheat flour (100%)

50g fine oatmeal (17%)

20g lard, dripping or butter (7%)

1 tsp bicarbonate of soda (1.5%)

½ tsp fine sea salt (1%)

1 tsp caster sugar (1.5%)

200g buttermilk at 20°C (67%)

200g whole milk at 20°C (67%)

30g oatbran (10%)

Michael Power, the baker for Ann Sutton at her bakery in New Ross, Co. Wexford, bakes large squares of tender salty-sweet soda bread in a frame, so that each blob of batter-soft dough spreads and is forced upward. This means the crumb stays tender and moist rather than dry, and the square form of the loaf gives usefully uniform slices. I have adapted his recipe, and added a trick from cake-baking to stop the bread peaking in the middle.

Preheat the oven to 210°C/410°F/gas mark 6½. Grease a deep, 17cm square cake tin with oil or melted butter and dust it liberally with extra wholewheat flour. Tear a sheet of aluminium foil to cover the top of the tin, and leave to one side.

In a large bowl, mix the flour with the oatmeal, then rub in the lard until the lumps have disappeared and the fat is evenly dispersed. Add the bicarbonate of soda, salt, and sugar, and toss through with your fingers.

In another bowl, combine the buttermilk and milk, then stir this through the flour mixture until you have a thick paste-like dough. Scrape well down to the bottom of the bowl to make sure all of the dry ingredients are mixed evenly through the liquid. Stir quickly: the soda will begin to react with the acid buttermilk as soon as they make contact, and you will need all of the gas produced to lift the loaf.

Sprinkle a little of the oatbran on to the base of the greased and floured tin, then scrape the dough into the tin and sprinkle the rest of the oatbran on top. Pat the dough down lightly so it sits in an even layer. Cover the top of the tin with foil.

Bake for 25 minutes, then remove the foil from the top and bake for a further 25 minutes. Leave to cool in the tin for a minute, then tip out on to a wire rack. When cool, wrap in waxed paper or freeze in a sealed container.

Denmark

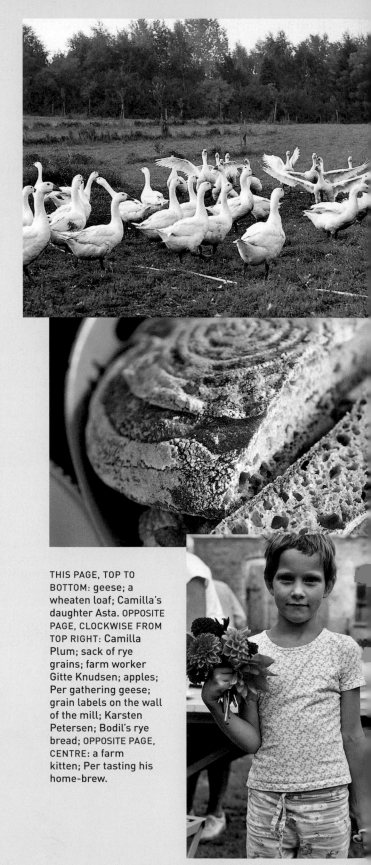

There is an air of nobility surrounding a woman who has reached a great age. Bodil Koelster is 76, with a smooth, golden tanned skin and studious lines that frame her calm face. It is late on a cool summer's day when she and her husband William arrive at Fuglebjerggaard, the home and organic farm run by her son Per Koelster and his partner, food writer Camilla Plum. The farm sits upon a slight hilltop in the northern fields of Zealand. Pink-painted outer walls of the old farm buildings face wheat and barley fields and slightly above, on the crest of the hill, graze steers and a few black-faced sheep. Bodil and William have spent the morning at their summer house, where they have picked a basket of ruddy, honey-fleshed mirabelles as a gift for the farm.

On the table sits a freshly baked loaf of rye bread, sharply cornered and dense with moist, plump rye grains, wrapped in an oiled paper bag to protect it as it matures – another gift from Bodil. We sit on old wooden farmhouse chairs gathered around the kitchen table. The sun is hidden behind a sky smooth with a blanket of cloud, lighting the dark wooden surface of the table strewn with coffee cups, bread and butter, and a bowl of freshly-cut flowers from Camilla's garden.

"Most people haven't got the time to bake these days," Bodil says as she unwraps the loaf. "It is perfect," she announces with no regret. "I've worked and tried to perfect the recipe and I think, looking at this loaf, that now it's right. See the bag? This is a tip I've just learned. Brush the loaf with rapeseed oil when it comes out of the oven. Also brush the brown paper bag with oil and, when the loaf is cool, wrap it tightly in the oiled bag. This keeps the loaf sweet and moist." I can smell the distinct aroma of sour rye, and it is indeed a beautiful, remarkable loaf. "When I married I could cook," says Bodil, "and as my mother was a good cook, I had recipes I could adapt from home. It seemed all we could buy at that time was very good bread. All bread was rationed, but at least it was good. You were allocated points to buy bread, but you could convert those to buy flour instead, which many people did. That's what my mother did – she would bake white bread, which you couldn't usually buy. And we'd bake cakes in the tin: plum cakes with raisins and cake spices such as *kummel* (caraway), light in colour and sweet; cakes with chocolate studded through them; or citrus cakes. My mother baked until she went to live in a home.

THIS PAGE, TOP TO BOTTOM: geese; a wheaten loaf; Camilla's daughter Asta. OPPOSITE PAGE, CLOCKWISE FROM TOP RIGHT: Camilla Plum; sack of rye grains; farm worker Gitte Knudsen; apples; Per gathering geese; grain labels on the wall of the mill; Karsten Petersen; Bodil's rye bread; OPPOSITE PAGE, CENTRE: a farm kitten; Per tasting his home-brew.

One of the last things she did, during that last week when she lived in her own house, was to bake a loaf. That was so important to her, and I guess it will be for me too.

"You know, you pick up recipes whenever you get the chance. The recipe for this rye bread was given to me by Per. A young woman he met when he was 25 taught him how to make this loaf, and he taught me," she says, "and in turn my recipe for a sweet yeast bread I used to make at Christmas, that Per loves, I've written down for Camilla."

Camilla Plum is a tall, powerful presence on the farm. She sits across from us at the table subdued from the day's work, the farmer's mountain of daily tasks that reappear as frequently as the rise of the sun. But with a Lutheran zest and respect for work, she rarely loses her humour or passion. Where does her respect for good baking come from? "My mother was the greatest influence on my cooking, and gave me my love of food. I remember in the 1970s she bought a flour mill and experimented with wholemeal breadmaking. Those breads," she says and laughs gently, "I got very sick of them. The dough for the wholemeal bread was mixed with a little honey, flour, yeast, water, and salt. This made a soft dough that would be placed in the tin immediately after mixing and then left to rise. During the sixties there was an encouragement by the government to get women into the workforce. In our society women were the keepers of traditions. While women were away the cooking stopped, and industry stepped in to fill the void with supermarkets and prepared foods. We were told the tasks we were used to doing – cooking, looking after children – were worthless.

"Remember, these women were, and still are, the bearers of Danish culture. In Denmark, as in most countries, the complications and demands of cheaper methods of food production affect the qualities of the bread we buy. Customers were persuaded to demand characteristics from these foods that would not naturally be present, as well as a level of convenience that is immodest and at times immoral. We have lost familiarity with how things were made and the association of effort with reward."

The following morning, the workers on the farm gather around this same table, once again spread with coffee cups, bread, sweet butter and blackcurrant jam. Besides Camilla, Per, and their children, there are eight others. Karsten Soenderskov Petersen, 22, is one of them. "I live in my parents' basement", he tells me. "Everybody in my family bakes", he says, almost in surprise when I ask my usual question. I encounter this reaction often here, as baking bread at home is so common that to not bake bread is unusual. "At home we need fresh bread every day, so we take it in turns baking in my parents' kitchen", he says.

Eva Hauch works at the office. We sit in the orchard joking about the proverbs that use bread and baking as a metaphor. "Sometimes when we see a big muscled guy we call him *stort brød* (big bread)", she laughs. Eva asks me when I am leaving. "I'm baking a loaf at the moment," she tells me. "It's still in the oven, but hopefully it will be ready to take out tomorrow". The loaf she is talking about is a dark traditional loaf of *rugbrød* (rye bread). "This *surdej* (sour leaven) comes from Bornholm. Back in Esrum, a friend of our neighbour gave me a small piece of this leaven. They tell me it's over a hundred years old. Many people tell me about these mythical leavens, kept like an heirloom and a part of their heritage. When the children were growing up I would bake with it regularly. Now my friend and I have given pieces of the leaven to other friends, and that sharing is a way of keeping the starter alive, a safeguard to maintain the tradition." She brings the loaf the next morning, carefully wrapped in white waxed paper neatly enclosed at either end with sharp paper folds, and slipped inside a tight clear plastic bag. "Don't eat it today", she warns, "as the crumb will be sticky and clay-like. Leave it for a few days to settle." And I do. It survives the flight without harm, and when I unwrap it on the kitchen table at home it looks perfect. Slightly domed on the upper surface, it has a dark almost chocolatey crust. When sliced, it has a soft waxen texture to the crumb. The flavour is a mixture of the traditional tang of rye, the sourness from the leaven and a strong aftertaste of licorice.

> "We demand a level of convenience that is immodest....We have lost familiarity with how things were made and the association of effort with reward."
> **CAMILLA PLUM**

Maize bread

I had been lost for an hour, walking around looking for a bakery equipment supplier on the grey outskirts of Turin in Piedmont, when I saw a garage with a coffee bar at the back and nipped inside. And there was this haven. No matter how hard the life of the Italian man, he always has a sensitivity and respect for the finer things in life. As the barman offered to fetch me a cab, I sat in the gentle quietness of this garage café, with a little music, a little espresso, some water and a small sandwich made with *pane di mais* (maize bread) and layered with *lardo*, fresh basil leaves, and a slice of ripe cold tomato. Here is that yellow bread, both humble and remarkable.

FOR THE POLENTA (makes 150g):

1 tsp olive oil

50g cornmeal

100g water

FOR THE DOUGH

150g polenta (either fresh or leftover) (30%)

260g water at 20°C (52%)

2½ tsp fresh yeast, crumbled (2%)

100g buttermilk at 20°C (20%)

150g maize flour (30%)

350g strong white flour (70%)

1¼ tsp fine sea salt (2%)

FOR THE POLENTA Take two large dinner plates, oil one with the olive oil and put it to one side. Place the cornmeal in a small saucepan with the water and bring to the boil, stirring constantly until it thickens into a lump that wraps itself to the stirring spoon. Immediately remove the pan from the heat and scrape the cornmeal on to the oiled plate, patting it out flat with the spoon. Cover it with the other plate, up-turned, and leave to cool.

FOR THE DOUGH Thoroughly break up the stiffened polenta in the water, together with the yeast and buttermilk. The easiest way to do this is in a blender, or you could just mash the polenta, yeast, and buttermilk carefully with a fork until you have a smooth paste, then whisk the water in a little at a time. The result should be lump free.

Mix the flours and salt in a bowl and add the polenta paste. Squidge the mixture together until you have a smooth, sticky dough, then leave covered for 5 minutes.

Rub 1 tsp of good olive oil on to the work-surface. Remove the dough from the bowl and place it on the oiled work-surface. Rub a little more oil on your hands, then gently knead the dough for 10 seconds. Round the dough back into a ball, then return to the bowl. Cover with a cloth and leave for 10 minutes.

Knead again on the work-surface for 10 seconds. Round the dough, return to the bowl, cover, and leave for 15 minutes. Keep the kneading quick and even, without breaking the surface of the dough, so that at all times it remains smooth and taut. Repeat the kneading three times at 15 minute intervals, so by the end of 1¼ hours it is smooth, well risen, gently blistered with air bubbles near the surface, and cool to the touch. Leave the dough in a bowl covered with a cloth for a further 30 minutes.

Rub a clean tea-towel with a handful of flour to stop the dough from sticking, and use it to line a 25cm diameter x 12cm deep bowl, or use a linen-lined basket if you have one. Knead the dough gently into a round ball, then place it seam-side-up into the cloth-lined bowl. Gently fold the ends of the cloth back over the top of the dough and leave to rise in a cool place for 1 hour.

Preheat the oven to 220°C/425°F/gas mark 7. Tip the dough out on to a floured tray and, using a sharp knife, cut a criss-cross pattern in the top of the loaf. Bake for 50–60 minutes, or until the loaf is brown and light in weight.

Crisp cornmeal sticks

The layering of soft folds of dough with butter, fat or oil, is not unique to puff pastry. The Indian *chapati* gains its flaky texture by being brushed with clarified butter, rolled, then sliced and rolled once more. The pastry for an Italian *sfogliatelle* is rolled ultra-thin, brushed with oil or butter, rolled up into a tube, then sliced thinly and folded around a sweet ricotta filling. In England, the eponymous fat of a lard cake is rolled through the dough to melt during baking. These sticks of bread dough use the same principle. A little onion cooked in butter is mixed with cornmeal and milk, just pushing the flavour over towards something savoury.

50g unsalted butter (17%)

110g onion, finely chopped (37%)

60g cornmeal (20%)

250g cold milk (83%)

140g white leaven (47%) (see pages 25–27)

¾ tsp fresh yeast, crumbled (2%)

300g strong white flour (100%)

1 tsp fine sea salt (2.5%)

12 tsp extra virgin olive oil (20%)

sea salt flakes

Melt the butter in a small saucepan and add the chopped onion. Heat gently over a low flame, with the lid on, for 3–4 minutes, until the onion has softened and become somewhat transparent.

Stir in the cornmeal and cook for 30 seconds. Add 100g of the milk and stir vigorously for 1 minute until the mixture thickens and comes away from the sides of the pan in a ball. Remove from the heat and tip into a large, cold bowl. Whisk in the remaining milk, followed by the white leaven and yeast. Add the flour and salt, then squeeze and stir with your hands until you have a thick, soft dough.

Lightly flour the work-surface and knead the dough for 10 seconds, then cover it with a tea-towel and leave for 5 minutes. Repeat the short kneading, cover the dough, and leave for a further 5 minutes.

Roll the dough out into a 27 x 35cm rectangle. Tip 2 tsp of extra virgin oil on to the dough, then rub or brush the oil so that it covers the surface. Fold the rectangle in by a third at each end. Lift the dough up, dust the work-surface with flour once more, then replace the dough and flour the top. Cover the dough with a tea-towel and leave for 5 minutes to relax.

Repeat the rolling, oiling, folding and flouring five more times, each time trying to roll the dough to the original dimensions. Remember to leave the dough to rest between rolling, to ensure that it does not tear. Roll the dough once more to 27 x 35cm, cover with a tea-towel, and leave for 40 minutes.

Preheat the oven to 220°C/425°F/gas mark 7. Line a baking sheet with aluminium foil, and rub it lightly with olive oil. Remove the tea-towel, and cut the dough into thin strips that will fit the length of your baking sheet, leaving room for the strips to expand. Sprinkle a few flakes of sea salt down the centre of each strip.

Place the tray in the centre of the oven and bake for 30 minutes, flipping the sticks over half-way through baking so that they colour evenly. Leave to cool on a wire rack.

You can eat these with thin slices of Parma ham wrapped around them, or use them to dip into a thick soup such as a minestrone.

Barley bread

Barley flour, when mixed with water, does not contain the glutinous, elastic protein that will stretch and hold gas inside the loaf. So although it was one of the earliest grains western man relied upon for sustenance, it was quickly left behind when we turned to leavened breads. This recipe uses the traditional flavour of barley in a modern and light-textured loaf.

TIP This recipe attempts to overcome the lack of gluten in barley by using toasted barley flour for flavouring while relying on white flour to keep the loaf light. Cooked whole barley grains are then added to the mixing liquid, held suspended by the gluten in the dough. You could soak these grains in wine, ale or sour milk to add flavour, but remember to drain them well.

100g barley flour (29%)

180g water at 20°C (52%)

200g white leaven (57%) (see pages 25–27)

50g honey (14%)

1 tsp fresh yeast, crumbled (1.5%)

240g cooked barley grains, rinsed until cold (69%)

250g strong white flour (71%)

1 tsp fine sea salt (2%)

Preheat the oven to 200°C/400°F/gas mark 6. Spread the barley flour in a thin layer over a baking tray and bake for 10–12 minutes, until lightly coloured.

In a large mixing bowl, stir together the water, leaven, honey, and yeast. When evenly combined, add the barley grains and stir again. Finally, add the toasted barley flour, white flour, and salt, and stir until you have a thick, sticky dough. Tip the dough on to a lightly oiled (with corn or olive oil) work-surface and knead for 10 seconds. Return to the bowl, cover with a tea-towel, and leave for 10 minutes.

Remove from the bowl, knead for 10 seconds, then return to the bowl and leave for 10 minutes. Give the dough a final knead and leave covered in the bowl for 1 hour.

Dust the work-surface with flour. Divide the dough into two equal pieces. Gently knead each piece for 10 seconds and into a ball. Cover and leave for 10 minutes, to give the dough time to relax. Rub a clean tea-towel with flour, so the dough doesn't stick to it, and lay across a large tray (or use long floured baskets).

Sit one ball of dough seam-side-upwards on the floured work-surface. To shape the dough (see page 20), pat it flat with your hands, then take the left and right sides furthest from you and fold them inwards towards the centre by 2cm, making a triangular point. Next, take that same point and fold it inwards to the centre, pressing it firmly down to seal. Rotate the dough 180°, and repeat with the other side. Rotate the dough once more, so that you are back in the starting position.

If you are right-handed, fold the dough in half towards you starting at the right-hand end, sealing the dough with the heel of your right hand while holding and folding the dough with your left. Roll the shaped loaf (with both hands tucked around it) on the work-surface, pressing down slightly more with the heel of each hand to give the ends a gentle point. Lift the dough and place it seam-side-upwards on the cloth. Finally, fold and pull the cloth up the sides of the loaf (or if using a flour-dusted basket, simply place the dough inside it seam-side upwards).

Repeat the shaping with the remaining piece of dough and sit this next to the first, separated by the floured cloth. Cover and leave in a warm (21°C) place for 1½ hours. Preheat the oven to 220°C/425°F/gas mark 7. Turn the dough seam-side-down on to a flour-dusted baking tray, then apply a fine spray of water. Bake in the centre of the oven for 50 minutes, or until the loaf is a light brown in colour and light in weight. Cool, then wrap in waxed paper.

Buckwheat pancakes

Buckwheat and oatmeal have a nutty flavour when baked on a griddle as a flatbread. Toast these grains, and this taste is enhanced to become slightly smoky. We often overlook pancakes, but as the first of the noble breads they suit so many of our simpler foods and deserve a closer look. Smoked fish and roe, served with a little sour cream, snipped chives and melted butter make for a great feast – especially when washed down with a shot of vodka or schnapps.

TIP The whole buckwheat grains soften very rapidly, so they have a delicate texture in the pancakes. Although these flatbreads contain whole grains, each bite is tender and soft.

50g boiling water (50%)

50g *kasha* (toasted buckwheat) (50%)

125g cold water (125%)

scant ½ tsp fresh yeast, crumbled (2.5%)

100g buckwheat flour (100%)

scant ½ tsp fine sea salt (2.5%)

175g cold milk (175%)

oil, lard or butter for cooking

Pour the boiling water over the *kasha*, and stir quickly so that the water is evenly absorbed (some kernels will pop open quickly while others will stay crunchy). Pour the cold water over the kernels. Crumble the yeast into the water and stir. Stir in the buckwheat flour until evenly combined, then add the salt and stir again thoroughy.

Cover the bowl and leave in a warm place for 1½ hours, by which time the batter should have risen slightly and a network of bubbles formed under the surface. Stir in the cold milk until you have a thin batter.

Preheat a non-stick frying pan, and 1 tsp of oil, lard or butter. Heat until it is almost smoking hot. The oil is important, even with the non-stick pan, as it helps crisp the edges of the pancakes and adds to their flavour.

Ladle 40–50g batter into the centre of the pan and swirl it so that the batter spreads thinly. Replace over the heat, and cook until the edges are crisp and brown and the surface broken with air bubbles – a minute or so. With a spatula, loosen the pancake from the frying pan and flip over. Cook for another minute, or until both sides are brown. Remove from the pan, place on a plate and cover with a cloth while you cook the remaining pancakes.

Serve warm with melted butter or sour cream and something like caviar or smoked fish, or as a sweet dish with honey and a squeeze of lemon.

Seeds
& grains

Sometimes we let our heads rule our hearts, and it isn't necessarily a good thing. My head imagines that what it likes is always good for me, but my heart needs food that respects my health. The unrefined grain, whole and complete with vitamins, minerals and fibre, can provide many of the nutrients my body will ever need. Breadmaking gets these good grains into an edible package.

F. Marian McNeill's *The Scots Kitchen* describes bound mixtures, for example of fish roe and oatmeal to make a type of fish "cake". These combine grains into a single form to extend, bulk out, and smooth strong flavours. Dry seeds, rarely palatable, are pleasant once moistened, combined, and cooked like this. The relationship between puddings, loaves, gruel, and stuffing is close; while we like to think of them as separate parts of a meal, the recipes for these foods have one shared goal: to cook grains into a form we enjoy.

The modern diet is about refinement, and the wide availability of refined food was a gift of the industrial age. With nothing brittle, coarse, hard or tough, everything in our processed food yields easily against our teeth – and usually doesn't require them! Refined, white grainless bread outsells any other sort throughout the world, though we know to live on refined carbohydrate is unhealthy. How do we turn this around? By incorporating wholegrains into the food we eat in a way we like, and by sharing this food with others.

Cooked, soaked wholegrains add a moist heartiness to any bread recipe. You can add up to 20 per cent cooked grains to the total flour weight of any bread recipe without needing to alter the other ingredients or quantities. To add more grains, you will need to tweak the recipe as the dough might need more leavening or a change to the water content. Do alter the grains suggested in these recipes to suit your taste or to use what you have available.

Five-grain loaf

My first encounter with a good wholegrain rye loaf was in the early 1980s, when I moved to London and stumbled across Neal's Yard, founded by the late Nick Saunders in the 1970s in a visionary move to create a wholefood refuge by the old flower and vegetable market in Covent Garden. The yard was in among old warehouses that kept it separate from the sprawl of the streets around and felt calm and tranquil. At that time I was living and cooking in an ashram in Notting Hill, and would trek there for vegetables and juice. The bakery at Neal's Yard was the home of the sturdy loaf, and this recipe is a nod of respect to those bakers who from the beginning practised and promoted organic breadmaking and the importance of sustainable, responsible living.

150g strong white flour (42%)

100g strong wholemeal flour (29%)

100g rye flour (29%)

1½ tsp fine sea salt (2%)

210g mixed, well-cooked grains, such
  as rice, lentils, rye or wheat) (60%)

50g whole millet (14%)

30g oatmeal (9%)

100g white leaven (29%) (see pages 25–27)

50g honey (14%)

25g molasses (7%)

150g water at 20°C (43%)

2½ tsp fresh yeast, crumbled (2.5%)

50g sunflower oil (14%)

oats or fine oatmeal, for finishing
  the loaf

In a large bowl, combine the three flours with the salt. In another bowl, mix the cooked grains, millet, and oatmeal with the leaven, honey, molasses, water, yeast, and oil, and beat well until combined. Pour this wet mixture in with the dry ingredients, and stir well until you have a soft, sticky dough. Scrape any dough from your fingers into the bowl, then cover and leave for 10 minutes.

Rub 1 tsp of corn or olive oil on the work-surface and knead the dough on the oiled surface for 10 seconds, ending with the dough in a smooth, round ball. Clean and dry the bowl, then rub lightly with a tsp of oil. Return the dough to the bowl, cover, and leave for a further 10 minutes. Remove the dough and knead once more on the oiled surface, returning the shape of the dough to a smooth, round ball. Place it back in the bowl, cover, and leave for 1 hour in a warm (21–25°C) place.

Lightly flour the work-surface and shape the dough into a baton (see page 21). Rub a tea-towel with a handful of flour (or use a linen-lined proving basket) and place the dough inside, seam-side-up. Wrap the dough up snugly in the cloth, and leave to rise for 1½ hours, or until almost doubled in height.

Preheat the oven to 210°C/410°F/gas mark 6½. Upturn the loaf on to a flour- or semolina-dusted tray, spray (or brush) the upper surface with water then sprinkle the surface of the loaf with oats or fine oatmeal. Using a sharp blade, slash the loaf diagonally two or three times. Bake in the centre of the oven for 30 minutes, then reduce the heat to 190°C/375°F/gas mark 5 and bake for a further 15–20 minutes until the loaf is a good brown, feels light in weight and sounds hollow when tapped on the base. Leave to cool on a wire rack.

Rolled oat and apple bread

Oats have remarkable properties when combined in breads and give the loaf a chewiness and moistness. If you read the ingredients for processed tray bakes and soft-bite biscuits, you'll often see oat flour listed because it can make foods taste richer without the need for so much oil or fat. Here, as with Swiss muesli, the oats are soaked in boiling water then mixed with grated apple. They ensure the bread stays moist and tender over several days.

TIP: Oats vary in quality. When Donnie McLeod cooked porridge for me one morning at his home in Inverness (see page 178), using locally grown organic oats with water and salt, the difference was extraordinary. It had none of that blandness associated with processed breakfast food – instead it had a complex, earthy flavour similar to rye.

50g rolled oats (20%)

100g boiling water (40%)

200g peeled and grated apple (80%)

75g water at 20°C (30%)

100g white leaven (40%)
  (see pages 25–27)

¾ tsp fresh yeast, crumbled (2%)

250g strong white flour (100%)

¾ tsp fine sea salt (2%)

egg wash (see page 187)

oats or fine oatmeal for finishing
  the loaf

Put the rolled oats into a small bowl and pour over the boiling water. Leave aside for 5 minutes while you prepare the other ingredients.

Add the grated apple to the water, leaven, and yeast. Stir the mixture well with a fork so that the yeast dissolves, then stir the soaked oats into this. In another bowl weigh the flour with the salt. Pour the wet ingredients into the flour and stir the mixture with your hands until it is evenly combined and you have a soft, sticky dough. Scrape any dough from your fingers into the bowl, then cover and leave for 10 minutes.

Rub 1 tsp of corn or olive oil on the work-surface and knead the dough on the oiled surface for 10 seconds, ending with the dough in a smooth, round ball. Clean and dry the bowl, then rub lightly with a tsp of oil. Return the dough to the bowl, cover, and leave for a further 10 minutes. Remove the dough and knead once more on the oiled surface, returning the shape of the dough to a smooth, round ball. Put it back in the bowl, cover and leave for 1 hour in a warm (21–25°C) place.

Lightly flour the work-surface and shape the dough into a baton (see page 21). Rub a tea-towel with a handful of flour (or use a linen-lined proving basket) and place the dough inside seam-side-up. Wrap the dough up snugly in the cloth, and leave to rise for 1½ hours, or until almost doubled in height.

Preheat the oven to 210°C/410°F/gas mark 6½. Upturn the loaf on to a flour- or semolina-dusted tray, then dust the surface of the loaf with oats or fine oatmeal. Bake the loaf in the centre of the oven for 30 minutes, then lower the heat to 190°C/375°F/gas mark 5 and bake for a further 15–20 minutes, until the loaf is a good brown, feels light in weight, and sounds hollow when tapped on the base. Leave to cool on a wire rack.

Wholegrain rye bread

This loaf is similar to the one baked by Bodil Koelster in Denmark, and typical of the type of wholegrain rye once common in that region. There is a certain grace to this bread, with its clean form unfussed by cuts or tricky ends. It is a simple rye bread, combining wholegrains and light flour with a clean acidic tang given by the hefty dose of leaven. I've added a little yeast, but if you have the time, and if your leaven is bright and active, make it without. You can simply cook and soak the rye grains in water, but I like the taste of a little bottle of real ale used for an overnight marinade.

TIP Like all 100 per cent rye breads, leave the loaf for a day (or even two), wrapped tightly in waxed paper, before slicing thinly. I like to serve this rye bread with cured fish and marinated vegetables, and like a good Roquefort, it is helped by a scraping of unsalted butter.

150g water at 20°C (60%)
200g rye leaven (80%)
   (see pages 25–27 and 31)
¼ tsp fresh yeast, crumbled (0.5%)

400g cooked and soaked rye grains
   (160%) (see page 49)
¾ tsp fine sea salt (0.5%)
250g light rye flour (100%)

Beat together the water, leaven, and yeast until evenly combined, then stir in the grains. In a larger bowl, mix the salt and rye flour together with your fingers, then pour in the grains and liquid. Squidge the mixture together until you have a very soft, sticky paste of a dough (the dough will be constrained by the sides of the tin). Scrape any dough from your fingers into the bowl, then cover and leave for 10 minutes.

Evenly oil and dust with rye flour a 20 x 10cm loaf tin. Scrape the dough from the bowl into the tin, then smooth down the top of the dough so that it sits flat in the tin. As the dough contains no elastic gluten to give it resilience, there is no benefit to giving it a first rise. Simply get it into the tin and let it rise once before baking. Cover the tin and leave the dough for 2½ hours, or until the loaf has risen in height by a third.

Preheat the oven to 210°C/410°F/gas mark 6½. Uncover the tin and prick the upper surface of the dough lightly with a fork. Bake the loaf in the centre of the oven for 20 minutes, then reduce the heat to 200°C/400°F/gas mark 6 and bake for a further 25–30 minutes. By this time the loaf should be a dark golden-brown on the upper surface and the dough should have pulled away slightly from the sides of the tin. Leave the loaf in the tin for 10 minutes to cool slightly. Using a blunt knife, carefully ease the loaf out on to a wire rack to finish cooling.

When the loaf is cool, lightly oil a brown paper bag and wrap the bread up snugly inside it. Store the loaf for at least two days, at a cool room temperature, before slicing thinly to serve.

Golspie loaf

Sometimes grains can simply form a crust on the loaf. Here, coarse-milled oatmeal lines the tin for a bread made with a soft, moist dough. I wrote this recipe at the historic Golspie watermill up in the Scottish highlands, where an old grain known as bere is still milled and used to make a type of flatbread known as a bere bannock. As wheat was always an important and valuable crop, the poor people would only have the less highly regarded oatmeal and bere barley to use for food. Now wheat has become far more common and ordinary, yet oatmeal and barley have dwindled in popularity except by those who value wholegrains in their diet. By combining the two, with the barley as the leaven and the oatmeal as the crust, a plain wheaten loaf becomes a nutritionally complex and satisfying bread.

250g water at 20°C (62%)

300g barley or rye leaven (75%)
  (see pages 25–27 and 31)

¾ tsp fresh yeast, crumbled (1%)

400g strong wholemeal flour (100%)

1 tsp fine sea salt (2%)

75g coarse oatmeal, for dusting the
  loaf (19%)

Whisk the water with the leaven and yeast. In a large bowl, toss the wholemeal flour with the sea salt, then stir in the liquid. Mix this until you have an evenly combined, soft and sticky dough. Scrape any dough from your fingers into the bowl, then cover and leave for 10 minutes.

Rub 1 tsp of corn or olive oil on the work-surface and knead the dough on the oiled surface for 10 seconds, ending with the dough in a smooth, round ball. Clean and dry the bowl, then rub lightly with a tsp of oil. Return the dough to the bowl and leave for a further 10 minutes. Remove the dough and knead once more on the oiled surface, returning the shape of the dough to a smooth, round ball. Place it back in the bowl, cover, and leave for 1 hour in a warm (21–25°C) place.

Rub a 20cm springform cake tin with oil. Sprinkle half the oatmeal evenly around the inside of the tin. Lightly flour the work-surface, and roll the dough into a disc measuring something just short of 20cm in diameter. Lift this up and press it into the tin. Using the knuckles of your hand, press the dough into the edges of the tin so that it sits evenly. Dust the upper surface of the dough with additional oatmeal. Cover the surface of the tin loosely with a cloth and leave in a warm (21–25°C) place for 1 hour, or until almost doubled in height.

Preheat the oven to 210°C/410°F/gas mark 6½. Score the dough with a deep cross, right through to the base of the tin. This will allow the bread to be broken into quarters after it has been baked. Bake in the centre of the oven for 25 minutes, then reduce the heat to 190°C/375°F/gas mark 5 and bake for a further 20 minutes, or until the loaf is a dark golden-brown on the upper surface. Remove from the oven, unclasp the tin, and remove the loaf to finish cooling on a wire rack.

Lentil rolls

The dry peppery taste of a lentil is suited to a light, rye-based dough, as the astringency of the rye lightens what might otherwise be a heavy flavour. The lentils are cooked until they are quite soft before being added to the dough so they combine well and bake moistly. Slightly sweet with a tender crumb, these dinner rolls are good with a broth-based soup such as cock-a-leekie or spring vegetable. Freeze them as soon as they're cold, in an airtight container, and reheat in an 180°C/350°F/ gas mark 4 oven for 10–12 minutes.

200g cooked Puy lentils, soft and drained (80%)

100g water at 20°C (40%)

1 tsp fresh yeast, crumbled (1.5%)

1½ tbsp runny honey (10%)

200g strong white flour (80%)

50g rye flour (20%)

¾ tsp fine sea salt (2%)

Beat the cooked lentils with the water, yeast, and honey, and leave to one side. In a large bowl combine the white and rye flours with the salt, then pour the yeast-liquid in. Mix until you have an evenly combined, soft and sticky dough. Scrape any dough from your fingers into the bowl, then cover and leave for 10 minutes.

Rub 1 tsp of corn or olive oil on the work-surface and knead the dough on the oiled surface for 10 seconds, ending with the dough in a smooth, round ball. Clean and dry the bowl, then rub lightly with a tsp of oil. Return the dough to the bowl, cover, and leave for a further 10 minutes. Remove the dough and knead once more on the oiled surface, returning the shape of the dough to a smooth round ball. Place it back in the bowl, cover, and leave for 1 hour in a warm (21–25°C) place.

Lightly flour the work-surface and roll the dough into a sheet measuring 25 x 20cm. Lay this sheet of dough on a tray lined with a flour-dusted cloth, then cover the surface of the dough with another cloth and leave for 1 hour, or until almost doubled in height.

Preheat the oven to 210°C/410°F/gas mark 6½. Uncover the dough and cut into 16 squares. Carefully lift the rolls up and place them on a flour-dusted baking tray, ensuring that the edges do not touch. Bake in the centre of the oven for 25 minutes, or until the tops of the rolls are golden brown and feel light.

Rice bread

Left-over rice, even if it's over-cooked but with the grains still separate, can be mixed into dough to make a sturdy, simple, white loaf. This loaf, which I enjoy toasted in the morning, uses milk and a little honey to slightly sweeten and help colour the crumb when toasted. This is important as the rice doesn't take colour very quickly.

TIP For the pictures I used an old-fashioned Pullman loaf tin. This has a sliding cover, producing a uniform loaf that gives you square slices. You can buy Pullman tins from specialist kitchen equipment suppliers. But no harm will come if you use an ordinary tin and let the top of the loaf pop up.

150g tender cooked rice (preferably short-grain) (60%)

150g milk at 20°C (60%)

1¼ tsp fresh yeast, crumbled (2%)

40g honey (16%)

250g strong white flour (100%)

¾ tsp fine sea salt (2%)

In a jug or bowl, whisk together the rice, milk, yeast, and honey. In a larger bowl, toss the flour and salt between your fingers, then pour the liquid in and mix until you have an evenly combined, soft and sticky dough. Scrape the dough from your fingers into the bowl, cover and leave for 10 minutes.

Rub 1 tsp of corn or olive oil on the work-surface and knead the dough on the oiled surface for 10 seconds, ending with the dough in a smooth, round ball. Clean and dry the bowl, then rub lightly with a tsp of oil. Return the dough to the bowl and leave for a further 10 minutes. Remove the dough and knead once more on the oiled surface, returning the shape of the dough to a smooth, round ball. Place it back in the bowl, cover, and leave for 1 hour in a warm (21–25°C) place.

Grease the inside of a 10 x 27cm Pullman loaf tin with a snug-fitting lid. If you can't get one, then use a slightly smaller tin and allow the dough to rise out of it. Shape the dough into a baton (see page 21), then place it in the tin seam-side-down. Slip the lid over the tin (or cover the dough with a cloth) and leave for 1 hour, or until almost doubled in height (or close to touching the lid).

Preheat the oven to 210°C/410°F/gas mark 6½. If your loaf is in a tin with a lid, simply place in the centre of the oven. If your loaf is in an open tin, dust the top with flour, then place it in the oven. Bake for 25 minutes, then reduce the heat to 190°C/375°F/gas mark 5 and bake for a further 20 minutes, or until the loaf has pulled away slightly from the sides of the tin and is a good golden-brown. Remove from the tin and leave to cool on a wire rack.

Germany

There are foods that remind us, very subtly, of flavours from our childhood. For me a fine bread-crumbed gratin, soft underneath with melting cheese, will always be, somewhere deep in my mind, cheese on toast. Our parents got in early and taught us, with a mixture of love and angst, what they thought was good. They gave us their personal best list – flavours that meant something to them. My father would cook tripe on Saturdays, and now, when I see tripe on a menu, my first thought is "my father would like that".

It is in the home that we get our first opportunity to learn about good food, and sharing a loaf that you have baked can help teach the people who you share your home with. Sharing home-baked bread encourages home-baking.

As often as she can, Julia Decker spends time writing down recipes that have been told to her by her father and grandmother. First she writes them on scraps of paper and post-it notes, then she transcribes them into a hardback book. As with many families, the recipes of Julia's relatives are remembered rather than written down, but having her own hand-written recipe book ensures that methods and techniques will stay close to her parents' and grandparents' intent when they are passed on to her children.

Julia's two-room apartment in Munich is small, with a kitchenette in which she bakes bread. She doesn't bake every day, but rather a few times a year. So she is a "sometime baker", someone who bakes a few times a year because it's a pleasure. Around the world there are lots of just this sort of baker: "sometimers" who dig out an old recipe and bake over a day to see how they fare.

During the 1980s in Germany, the organic and Demeter (an association that encourages farmers to view the soil as a living thing) movements became prominent in food retailing, and bakers who promoted wholegrain breads became popular. The best word to describe the crumb of these loaves is "compact" – they are like a grain terrine studded with moist whole grains of rye, wheat, spelt or linseed. The grains combine to give flavour and texture, and with other seeds mark the flavour territory that is represented by each baker.

Chains such as the excellent Hopfpfisterei and Fritz-Mühlenbäckerei, as well as independent bakers, who sell at the Viktualien outdoor market, supply remarkable breads rich with seeds and grains without

ABOVE, CLOCKWISE FROM TOP: a street in central Munich; Julia Decker as a child with her father on a donkey in Greece; baker Franz Stricker holds salt-crusted crescent rolls; Stricker's coriander seed bread; OPPOSITE, CLOCKWISE FROM TOP LEFT: wholemeal Demeter bread at the Viktualien market in central Munich; handfuls of soft dough; Stricker holding a typical Bavarian dark rye bread; a loaf from the Hopfpfisterei bakery; spiced *vinschgauer schüttelbrot* from the southern Tyrol; Stricker's lye-dipped and baked pretzels; Stricker's wooden-basket-proved rye bread; Julia compiles her family's recipes; a young Julia, with the blonde hair, makes sandwiches with her school friend Philipp; Julia in her Munich apartment.

Mit Philipp auf Fehmarn

"At Franz Stricker's store... the old
electric oven was built in the 1950s,
yet is kept gleaming like a loved car."

Baker Franz
Stricker with
his oven.

a stack of unusual rye flatbreads in a window. The
bakery is open, and the baker Franz Stricker is there.
His little store has a gentle disorder about it, with bags
of biscuits and cut sandwiches and, behind the
counter, racks sparsely lined with the week's last
remaining loaves.

Franz invites me to see the ovens, so we exit through
the back of the shop into a small courtyard and across to a
door on the other side. The door leads to a narrow spiral
staircase that decends into the basement where, tucked
away at the back of another building, is his bakery. The
space is lined with wooden shelves, and from the ceiling
hang the peels, brooms and long scrapers that are the
ovenman's tool kit. Light streams in through windows that
open out on to a light well, and between these windows is
a well-used wooden bench, where scrapers and brushes
are kept in a small pot.

Franz explains how some of the other breads are
baked. "Here", he says, carefully lifting the lid on a
large oblong tray, "is the lye dip for the pretzels,
which is the best way to get that dark red colour on
the crust". Around from that is the old electric oven,
built in the 1950s yet kept gleaming like a loved car.
He races around, getting other loaves out to photograph,
most of which have spices such as coriander, aniseed or
fennel or fragrances such as lemon or orange zest in the
rye dough.

Franz explains how the flatbread I'd seen in the
window is made. "I toss it between two sheets of
board", he says, "back and forward until the constant
slapping flattens it." This traditional bread from the
southern Tyrol is called *vinschgauer schüttelbrot*. It is
almost all crust, and resembles a large savoury biscuit,
being quite crisp and dry. The recipe is unusual, using rye
flour, rye leaven, water, salt, and a hefty dose of fennel,
anise and citrus zest.

I ask Franz what will happen to his recipes. "They
end here", he says, holding his arms out in the room,
"I'm 56, and there is no-one to pass the recipes on to.
This is where I bake and this is where the recipes will
probably stay."

even the slightest nod towards white softness. But
still these bakeries also sell ingredients for home-
baking – sachets of leaven, whole grains, flour, and sea
salt – and they promote themselves as centres for baking
excellence rather than simply as retailers of their own
good loaves.

Prior to this change, finding good bread in Germany was
not so easy. "When my brother and I were young", says
Julia, "there was no possibility of buying good bread, so
my father started to bake bread at home: bread with taste,
not like white toast." We knead dough together on the
bleached wooden table, and we talk about her father's
bread. "It was really good, made with a grain that we call
dinkel, but that you call spelt, which has a rich nutty taste.
It is still the flour I use when I bake.

"There is a famous German cookbook writer, who wrote
a book about baking in which he included a recipe
inspired by the bread my father used to bake. My
surname is Decker, so he called it *deckerspeziellbröt*, which
means 'Decker's special bread'. My father always made
this kind of bread, and in the early 1980s it was unusual to
bake bread at home."

Not all recipes get noted and recorded, though.
Sometimes a baker's work is a performance that only
remains as a memory after the baker and bread have
gone. Walking down Klenzestraße, a tiny side street
in the down-town district off the Gärtnerplatz, I notice

Sunflower bread

This is a very simple quick loaf to make, jam-packed with toasted sunflower seeds and with a slight taste of honey. Toasting the seeds makes them taste almost nut-like.

200g strong white flour (80%)

50g millet flour (20%)

200g sunflower seeds, lightly
   toasted (80%)

¾ tsp fine sea salt (2%)

50g runny honey (20%)

100g white leaven (40%)
   (see pages 25–27)

¾ tsp fresh yeast, crumbled (1%)

100g water at 20°C (40%)

beaten egg or milk, for glazing
   the loaf prior to baking)

In a large bowl, combine the strong white and millet flours with the toasted sunflower seeds and salt. In another bowl or jug, whisk the leaven with the honey, yeast, and water. Pour the liquid in with the dry ingredients, and stir well until you have an evenly combined, soft and sticky dough. Scrape any dough from your fingers, then cover the bowl and leave for 10 minutes.

Rub 1 tsp of corn or olive oil on the work-surface and knead the dough on the oiled surface for 10 seconds, ending with the dough in a smooth, round ball. Clean and dry the bowl, then rub lightly with a tsp of oil. Return the dough to the bowl and leave for a further 10 minutes. Remove the dough from the bowl and knead once more on the oiled surface, returning the shape to a smooth, round ball. Place it back in the bowl, cover, and leave for 1 hour in a warm (21–25°C) place.

Lightly flour the work-surface and shape the dough into a ball (see page 21). Rub a tea-towel with a handful of flour and place the dough inside, seam-side-up. Wrap the dough up in the cloth, then place this inside a 2-litre deep, round bowl. This will help force the dough to rise upwards rather than spread outwards and give height to the dough. Leave it to rise for 1½ hours, or until almost doubled in height.

Preheat the oven to 210°C/410°F/gas mark 6½. Upturn the loaf on to a flour-dusted tray, then brush the loaf with beaten egg. Cut a deep cross in the centre of the loaf. Bake in the centre of the oven for 30 minutes, then lower the heat to 190°C/375°F/gas mark 5 and bake for a further 15–20 minutes, until the loaf is a good brown colour, feels light in weight, and sounds hollow if tapped on the base. Cool on a wire rack.

Linseed and wheat bread

Linseed (or flax seed, as it is otherwise known) is commonly found in mixed seed breads in Germany. A very important seed in European folk medicine, it was reputed to encourage healing if made into a paste and spread over a wound as a poultice. It contains high levels of alpha-linolenic acid, an essential fatty acid that must form part of our diet if we are to remain alert and healthy. A little linseed each week will only do the body good.

TIP But like all heavy-grain breads, I prefer a little often, so I've shaped this loaf into a stick that cuts into thin, bite-sized disks. Serve with a scraping of butter and a little berry jam.

150g strong white flour (60%)

100g strong wholemeal flour (40%)

¾ tsp fine sea salt (2%)

100g golden linseed (40%)

2 tsp ground malt powder (5%)
(see page 38–39)

150g water at 20°C (60%)

1 tsp fresh yeast, crumbled (2%)

In a large bowl, combine the two flours with the salt, linseed, and malt powder. In another bowl or large jug, whisk the water with the yeast. Pour the liquid in with the dry ingredients, and with your fingers squidge the two together until you have an evenly combined, soft and sticky dough. Scrape any dough from your fingers back into the bowl, cover and leave for 10 minutes.

Rub 1 tsp of corn or olive oil on the work-surface. Knead the dough on the oiled surface for 10 seconds, ending with the dough in a smooth, round ball. Clean and dry the bowl, then rub lightly with a tsp of oil. Return the dough to the bowl and leave for a further 10 minutes. Remove the dough and knead once more on the oiled surface, returning the shape of the dough to a smooth, round ball. Place it back in the bowl, cover, and leave for 1 hour in a warm (21–25°C) place.

Divide the dough into two even pieces, then shape each into a baton (see page 21). Leave these dough pieces on the work-surface for 10 minutes, covered lightly with a cloth. Roll each one out still further, into a sausage shape 30cm long. Place these on a flour-dusted tray, then cover with a cloth and leave for 1 hour, until doubled in height.

Preheat the oven to 210°C/410°F/gas mark 6½. Uncover the dough and brush the upper surface of each stick lightly with water. Bake in the centre of the oven for 25 minutes, then reduce the heat to 190°C/375°F/gas mark 5 and bake for a further 20 minutes, or until the loaves are golden brown and feel light in weight. Leave to cool on a wire rack.

Griddled buckwheat muffins

An English muffin is a twice-cooked bread, baked on the griddle then split and toasted on the fire. The honeycomb texture of a good muffin is suited to runny, dripping foods, such as soft poached eggs with melted butter, or warm hollandaise over wilted spinach. The muffin catches the sloppy stuff, which wets the crisp, toasted surface. As buckwheat cooks quickly and plumps within minutes of being soaked with hot water, it is well suited to a soft dough like this.

TIP If you want the muffins to toast quickly, try adding a little sugar to the dough, either in the form of honey or syrup (1 tbsp is enough), or replace half the water with milk. This will make sure they colour extra quick and stay soft. I prefer a crunchier toasted muffin so I leave the sweetening out.

100g boiling water (29%)

75g toasted buckwheat (22%)

2 tbsp cider vinegar (9%)

350g strong white flour (100%)

1 tsp fine sea salt (2%)

200g water at 20°C (57%)

¾ tsp fresh yeast, crumbled (1.5%)

25g melted butter (7%)

Pour the boiling water over the buckwheat, then add the cider vinegar and stir. Leave for 5 minutes for the buckwheat to slightly swell and absorb the water.

In a large bowl, combine the flour and salt. In another bowl, stir the soaked buckwheat with the water and yeast, then add this to the flour. Mix the dough together quickly and evenly until you have a soft, sticky mixture. Next, pour over the warm melted butter and work this evenly into the dough. Scrape any dough from your fingers into the bowl, then cover and leave for 10 minutes.

Rub 1 tsp of corn or olive oil on the work-surface and knead the dough on the oiled surface for 10 seconds, ending up with a smooth, round ball. Clean and dry the bowl, then rub lightly with a tsp of oil. Return the dough to the bowl and leave for a further 10 minutes. Knead the dough once more on the oiled surface, returning it to a smooth round ball. Return the dough to the bowl, cover, and leave for 1 hour in a warm (21–25°C) place.

Lightly flour the work-surface, then roll the dough out into a 25cm x 20cm rectangle about 2cm thick. Using a round 10cm cutter, cut discs from the dough and lay them on a flour-dusted tray or cloth. Continue with the remainder of the dough, re-rolling any scraps and cutting more to finish. Cover the muffins with a cloth and leave in a warm (20–25°C) place for 45 minutes to rise.

Take a large frying pan, ideally one with a close-fitting lid. Shake a little extra flour lightly over the muffin then, using a spatula, carefully transfer the muffins to the dry pan, three or four at a time. Cover the pan and leave over a gentle heat for 5 minutes, peeking underneath the muffins after a few minutes to see if the heat needs to be turned up or down. The trick is to let them cook for 5 minutes per side, adjusting the heat accordingly. If you cook them for too short a time, the muffins will be doughy and uncooked in the middle; too long a time, and the muffins will be dry. Once one side is cooked, carefully flip them over and cook on the other side. When they're done, remove and cool on a wire rack, then continue to cook the remaining muffins. When they're cold, store in a paper bag or freeze.

Abundant
harvest

There is a small apple tree in a large pot in our garden, rescued from under the shade of a grapevine. It was stunted from lack of sunlight, so I dug it up and put it in the pot so it could be moved around the garden to follow the sun. The tree is a James Grieve, an English variety popular in the late 19th-century for its sweet juice and fragrance. For a few years, the tree budded with pink blossoms which dropped off without fruiting. But after the third year, two small apples appeared, and I watched their progress daily, brushing off the greenfly and stopping the cats from biffing them. After a burst of late summer rain, one fell off green and hard; the other withered under an attack from wasps.

Down the road, by Merton Abbey mills where William Morris printed fabric, many old apple trees grow in the gardens of the houses that surround the supermarket plonked on the site of the medieval priory. There were once orchards, but now only these trees in people's gardens remain. Last summer, I walked by the stream to the mill and on the wall outside one house was a bag of apples next to a sign that read: "Please take – for free." Each day I walked there, those same apples sat untouched while the supermarket heaved with bag-laden trolleys. No one took the apples. Eventually, they shrivelled.

Every year, mature fruit trees produce an abundance of ripe apples, with one tree producing more than one family can use. What can you do with this free fruit? Juice some, make pies with a butter-rich crust, brew a simple scrumpy, peel and cook them long and slow until only a dark concentrate remains, sun-dry even more to use during the winter months. You might use apple flesh to stud a simple dough, and mix the juice with the leavening. Whatever you have an excess of, make it useful and a blessing. Use the fruit of the harvest in every possible way: this is kitchen economy and good living.

Spotted soda bread

Sometimes called spotted dick, this plain cake-like loaf is sold in the south of Ireland and, when fresh, has a creamy taste and a slight sweetness to the crumb. Though the crust is quite crisp for the first couple of hours after baking, it soon settles to something softer, like a fruit cake crust. This recipe contradicts the generosity of others in this chapter, as the currants are there to "spot" the bread, reflecting its frugal origins. Adding more fruit is simply not done. Well, not in a normal home, as my mother would say. Choose to add more at your peril.

TIP Eat this in slices as you would a scone – freshly baked with a little butter and a good preserve.

300g plain flour (100%)

½ tsp sea salt (1%)

2 tsp baking powder (3%)

50g butter (17%)

250g milk at 20°C (84%)

50g golden syrup (17%)

50g currants or sultanas (17%)

Oil and flour the inside of a 12x18cm oblong tin. Preheat the oven to 210°C/410°F/gas mark 6½.

In a large bowl, combine the flour, salt, and baking powder, then rub in the butter until the mixture resembles fine breadcrumbs. In another bowl or a jug, whisk the milk with the golden syrup until combined. Drop the currants or sultanas into this to wet them, then pour the liquid mixture into the dry ingredients and mix. Scrape the batter into the prepared tin.

Smooth the top of the batter down lightly with a spatula, and loosely cover the top of the tin with foil. Bake in the centre of the oven for 20 minutes, then remove the foil and bake for a further 20 minutes, or until the top of the bread is a good golden-brown. Remove from the oven, leave for a few minutes to cool and firm, then carefully remove the bread from the tin and leave to cool on a wire rack.

Raisin and cinnamon loaf

Fruited bread should be just that: bread so thick with rich, plump fruit that some inevitably breaks through the outer surface of the dough, no matter how carefully it is shaped. There are bakers who would reduce the amount of fruit to preserve the appearance but they, luckily, don't have to eat what they make. The complaint I frequently hear from customers is that the fruit and nut breads they buy seem mean. Now, although bakers must struggle to make a bread that doesn't punish their profits, this dilemma shouldn't affect the home baker. Produce the food you want to make, exactly the way you want to eat it.

TIP I can hear the voice of one baker I used to work with saying, "What? 50% raisins! Far too much!" Percentages explain how to achieve the best results. If you only have a few raisins, halve the other ingredients and make a smaller loaf.

OPPOSITE PAGE, FROM TOP LEFT:
1 The shaped loaf
2 The risen loaf on the tray.
3 The baked loaf.
4 The sliced loaf.

300g strong white flour (75%)
75g rye flour (19%)
25g wholewheat flour (6%)
1 tsp fine sea salt (2%)
½ tsp ground cinnamon (0.5%)
150g rye leaven (38%)
  (see pages 25–27 and 31)

150g water at 20°C (38%)
50g olive oil (13%)
1 tsp fresh yeast, crumbled (1%)
25g honey (6%)
200g raisins (50%)

Combine the three flours with the salt and cinnamon. In another bowl, whisk the leaven, water, olive oil, and yeast with the honey and raisins (I add the raisins to the liquid as the moisture helps the dough stick to them – some recipes suggest adding them later, but this only really applies to aggressive machine-mixing; hand-mixing is gentle and will not tear the fruit). Combine the wet mixture with the dry ingredients and stir with your hands to make an evenly combined dough. Scrape any dough from your fingers into the bowl, cover, and leave for 10 minutes.

Rub 1 tsp of corn or olive oil on the work-surface and knead the dough on the oiled surface for 10 seconds, ending with the dough in a smooth, round ball. Clean and dry the bowl, then rub lightly with a tsp of oil. Return the dough to the bowl and leave for a further 10 minutes. Remove the dough and knead once more on the oiled surface, returning the shape of the dough to a smooth, round ball. Place it back in the bowl, cover, and leave for 1 hour in a warm (21–25°C) place.

Lightly flour the work-surface and gently knead and shape the dough into a ball (see page 21). Using your fingers or your elbow (the baker's traditional method), dig down into the dough to make a hole through the centre. Then work the dough outwards with your hands until you have a large ring. Place this on a tea-towel that has been dusted with rye flour and laid across a dinner plate. Pluck the towel through the hole and pull it up a little to stop the loaf from closing in too much. Cover the dough ring with another tea-towel, and leave in a warm (21–25°C) place for 2 hours, or until doubled in height.

Preheat the oven to 210°C/410°F/gas mark 6½. Upturn the dough on to a semolina-dusted tray, peeling off the cloth so that the ring of dough sits bare. Using a sharp scalpel, cut around the circumference of the dough near the top of the loaf, making an incision about 5mm deep. Lightly spray the surface of the loaf with a mist of water, then bake in the centre of the oven for 50 minutes, or until the loaf is a good dark brown and feels relatively light in weight. Leave to cool on a wire rack.

1 2
3 4

Fruited barm cake

Though this fruit loaf can be made with a yeasted dough or any simple plain bread dough, I prefer it made with a barm-leavened dough. This adds a dark maltiness, which is often imitated in chemically-leavened recipes by soaking the fruit in ale or tea. Though that can produce a beautiful result, this recipe both teaches you how to add ingredients to a kneaded dough and produces a slightly different, traditional result, with a bread-like, rather than cake-like, texture.

500g dough (from page 41) (100%)

50g unsalted butter, very soft but not melted (10%)

1 medium egg (12%)

50g plain flour (10%)

50g dark brown sugar (10%)

50g currants (10%)

50g sultanas (10%)

zest of ½ orange (2%)

½ tsp fine sea salt (0.5%)

After the dough has been mixed and briefly kneaded (lightly, three times during the first 30 minutes), return it to the bowl. Add the soft butter – this is a time when you do not want to be disturbed; your hands will be very sticky. Squidging the dough through your fingers in a clenching motion, work the butter into the dough, breaking the dough gently so the butter is forced into it. Beat the egg and add this to the dough. Work the dough again with your fingers until it is almost combined but still somewhat rough.

Mix the flour, sugar, dried fruit, orange zest, and salt, then tip this on to the dough. Work the dough until it is evenly combined. Scrape any dough from your fingers into the bowl, cover and leave for 10 minutes. Give the dough two more light kneads, each 10 minutes apart, on an olive-oiled surface, then cover the dough in the bowl and leave to rise for 2 hours.

Oil and flour a 18cm square loaf tin. Shape the dough into a ball (see page 21) and press this seam-side-down into the tin with your knuckles so that it sits flat and even. Cover the tin with a cloth and leave the dough to rise in a warm (25°C) place for 4 hours, or until the loaf has doubled in height.

Preheat the oven to 200°C/400°F/gas mark 6. Uncover the loaf and bake in the centre of the oven for 20 minutes, then lower the heat to 180°C/350°F/gas mark 4 and bake for a further 20 minutes, covering the top of the loaf with foil towards the end of baking if the loaf looks dark. Remove the tin from the oven, leave to cool and firm for a minute, then carefully remove the loaf from the tin and leave to cool on a wire rack.

Prune and rye babas with Armagnac syrup

Don't think that bread must always precede a meal; it can create the finale. These little prune babas are a dessert bread for when the pudding follows something light and refreshing, such as grilled fish, tender young lettuce, and a fresh tomato salad. At the Relais Plaza, a beautiful restaurant placed on the corner of the Hotel Plaza Athénée, pâtissier Nicolas Berger serves a perfect plain baba, split in a silver bowl, just barely warm and drenched in syrup. Next to it sits another silver bowl filled with the softest whipped cream flavoured with vanilla and flecked with the odd brown scrape from the pod. Between the two sits a tiny porcelain jug of dark rum. You combine the three as you wish.

TIP This recipe will make 12 babas, and may exhaust your moulds. The best solution is to use some of the dough to make a *pain aux pruneaux* in a loaf tin, in addition to babas, and either freeze this after baking or use it in a dessert.

A prune is nothing other than a dried ripe plum, though as a child I was convinced the droopy black skin contained a certain horror. Now, I savour a good prune and its concentrated flavour. Look for soft, moist prunes and use them just as they are.

FOR THE SYRUP:

250g caster sugar

500g water

FOR THE BABAS:

200g strong white flour (80%)

50g light rye flour (20%)

¾ tsp fine sea salt (2%)

80g rye leaven (32%)

   (see pages 25–27 and 31)

100g milk at 20°C (40%)

3 medium egg yolks (36%)

60g castor sugar (24%)

2½ tsp fresh yeast, crumbled (6%)

100g unsalted butter, softened (40%)

200g soft prunes, pitted (80%)

FOR SERVING:

1 measure of Armagnac for each baba

double cream, whipped to soft peaks

FOR THE SYRUP Bring the sugar and water to the boil. Remove from the heat and leave to cool.

FOR THE BABAS In a large bowl, combine the strong white flour, rye flour, and salt. In another bowl, beat together the rye leaven, milk, egg yolks, sugar, and yeast. Pour the wet ingredients into the dry and mix until you have a soft, sticky dough. Scrape any dough from your fingers, cover with a cloth and leave for 10 minutes.

Slice the butter into thin pieces and allow to soften. Spread these on top of the dough and work them roughly into it. Tip the dough out on to the work-surface and work it gently and evenly for 5 minutes, until the butter is combined and the dough is smooth. The buttery dough will be quite sticky, but don't worry. Scrape the dough up and place in the refrigerator in a tightly covered large container that allows the dough enough room to rise slowly overnight.

The next day, cut the prunes into quarters. Lightly flour the work-surface and roll out the dough until it measures 30 x 50cm. Lay the prunes evenly over two-thirds of the dough, then fold the dough in by thirds. With a rolling pin, knock the dough flat, then fold it in by thirds again. Tap the dough with the rolling pin to seal it, then put back in the bowl and refrigerate for 1 hour.

Lightly grease and flour 12 baba moulds. Roll out the dough until it is 2cm thick and cut it into 5cm squares. For each piece, pinch the corners of the dough together to seal them, creating a ball of dough and avoiding getting air pockets trapped in the centre. Flip the ball over and press into the prepared mould. Cover with a cloth and leave to rise in a warm (25°C) place for 2 hours, or until doubled in height.

Preheat the oven to 200°C/400°F/gas mark 6. Place the babas on a tray and bake in the centre of the oven for 15 minutes, then reduce the heat to 180°C/350°F/gas mark 4 and bake for a further 20 minutes, or until the babas are a good brown colour. Leave to settle in their moulds for a minute, then ease the babas carefully from the moulds with a knife.

Serve warm, split open lengthways, with the syrup spooned over them, together with a little cream and Armagnac. A baba is best left to slightly stale, as it will hold its shape better when later soaked in syrup.

Cherry, fennel, and rye loaf

The cherry used to be an important tree in small communities. Not only were dyes made from the bark and roots, but the thick resin could be chewed as a gum to soothe the throat. The beautiful wood could be fashioned into tables and chairs. And the fruit – well, you already know their rich, tart flavour. At www.treesforlife.org.uk, a charity dedicated to preserving the Caledonian forests, the writer Paul Kendall describes how the wild gaen tree, a type of cherry, had a mysterious place in highland folklore: "…to encounter one was considered auspicious and fateful". In this loaf, a lot of dried cherries are mixed with fennel and rye in the dough and combined with whole rye grains that have been cooked and soaked overnight. It is good sliced and served with soft cheese, liver sausage and pickles.

TIP A little cherry brandy, or even Swedish cherry wine, can be used to soak the grains overnight.

150g strong white flour (60%)

100g fine rye flour (40%)

¾ tsp fine sea salt (2%)

2 tsp fennel seeds (4%)

100g rye leaven (40%)

(see pages 25–27 and 31)

125g water at 20°C (50%)

¾ tsp fresh yeast, crumbled (1%)

125g dried cherries, pitted (50%)

100g cooked and soaked rye grains (40%)

(see page 49)

white poppy seeds for dusting

In a large bowl, combine the white and rye flours with the salt and fennel. In another bowl, whisk the leaven with the water and yeast, then stir in the cherries and rye grains. Pour this mixture into the dry ingredients, and squidge everything together with your hands until you have a soft, evenly combined dough. Scrape any dough from your fingers into the bowl, cover and leave for 10 minutes.

Rub 1 tsp of corn or olive oil on the work-surface and knead the dough on the oiled surface for 10 seconds, ending with a smooth, round ball. Clean and dry the bowl, then rub lightly with a tsp of oil. Leave the dough in the bowl, covered, for a further 10 minutes. Remove the dough, knead once more on the oiled surface, returning the shape of the dough to a smooth, round ball. Return it to the bowl, cover, and leave for 1 hour in a warm (21–25°C) place.

Lightly flour the work-surface. Remove the dough from the bowl and form it into a baton (see page 21). Lay it on a semolina-dusted tray to rise for 1½ hours, covered loosely with a cloth.

Preheat the oven to 220°C/425°F/gas mark 7. Uncover the dough and spray the top of the loaf lightly with water. Sprinkle the top of the loaf with poppy seeds then make a cut along the length of the loaf. Bake in the centre of the oven for 25 minutes, then reduce the heat to 200°C/400°F/gas mark 6 and bake for a further 20 minutes, or until the bread is a good dark brown colour and feels light in weight. Leave to cool on a wire rack.

This recipe is also good for making two smaller loaves, perhaps one for immediate use and the other for freezing. Simply divide the dough into two equal parts, form each into a baton, then proceed with the rising and baking as described above.

Ireland

Flying back from Ireland, I sat in the departure lounge next to a young man who was returning to England to visit relatives. He told me how his father had left his city career years before and found a piece of land on a hill by a river, where he built his own house. He'd carried and mortared every brick, having dug the foundations by himself with a spade, and then placed every tile on the roof with his bare hands. He ploughs and thoughtfully farms his land, keeping it organic and sustainable, and tends a garden filled with vegetables and fruit trees, as well as keeping chickens, goats, and pigs. When the young man asked me where I'd been, I said I'd been staying with William Sutherland and Angela Ashe, at the School for Sustainable Living in Killowen. "You've been there?" he gasped, a touch awestruck. "They are my father's heroes."

To explain about the school, I must tell you about its founder, John Seymour. A 20th-century hero, Seymour is a passionate campaigner and activist for a way of life that is respectful of the land and of others, and his actions and battles place him far above the words of many of his contemporaries and allies. He believed, with extraordinary foresight, many years ago, that all was not well as we happily ravaged and consumed the Nature that is around us. He saw that unless we changed our way of life the consequences for this earth would be devastating. Decades later, we now know that Seymour was right.

The school is on a farm that was built by John, William, and Angela, situated up above the banks of the River Barrow, a mile down a long dirt track. It is a small, simple home, and it is against the family background of their childrens' daily life that lessons are taught, old ways explained, and home-keeping methods practised.

Baking bread is essential to this family life, and they make a wholegrain soda bread with a moist sturdy crumb. As William measures the ingredients and places them in an earthenware bowl, he explains the reaction of the students to a life devoid of processed foods. "They're surprised by the fussiness," he says. "Food is a living, biological thing, and whether you are growing crops or baking bread, each step you take should be considered and thoughtful."

Into the bowl go oats, wholewheat flour, eggs, and milk, to be mixed into a paste that resembles thick muesli. "We

THIS PAGE, TOP TO BOTTOM: beating eggs for soda bread; the view over Wexford from Slieve Coillte in the John F. Kennedy memorial park; the woodhut in William and Angela's garden. OPPOSITE, CLOCKWISE FROM TOP LEFT: rolled oats and flour; the bowl scraped clean; soda bread; wrapped halves of bread at The Bakehouse; baker Michael Power holding spotted soda bread; loaves and potatoes baking in William Sutherland's Stanley stove; swiss chard after the frost; soda bread dough being scooped into the tin. CENTRE: William Sutherland, his dog and his soda bread.

"Michael Power's... dough, made with wholewheat flour, buttermilk, soda, salt, and sugar, is so soft that it is almost like a batter."

make cider from our own apples," William says, scraping the dough into oblong loaf tins. "We put a cultured yeast in with the juice and get a reliable cider. It's wonderful how you put this murky brown liquid in and out comes this golden, crystal-clear, fermented cider. But again, because people are used to the filtered, pasteurized stuff, they come in and shake the bottle, which disturbs the layer of natural sediment at the bottom, so then we have to lay the bottle down and leave it to rest and settle again." The bread tins are placed in the Stanley stove together with a few scrubbed potatoes for our lunch, making use of the heat to cook them both simultaneously.

In New Ross, the bright yellow painted Bakehouse bakery sits up on North Street, a gentle slope through the centre of the town. New Ross is an old port town, but now only relics such as the towering flour silos from an old mill give a hint to its industrial past. Its warehouses now contain apartments. There is a replica of the SS Dunbrody in the harbour, the ship that took immigrants to America, and the town is now a destination for tourists returning to John F. Kennedy's great-grandfather's birthplace in nearby Dunganston. Ann Sutton, the owner of The Bakehouse, shows me the working area of the bakery. An oven, an old upright mixer, a stainless-steel table and wooden baking frames are the core of the bread-baking. Cakes, tarts, small pies, and rich dark fruit cakes help the trade along.

The following morning, baker Michael Power teaches me the knack of soda bread baking, his way. His dough, made with wholewheat flour, buttermilk, soda, salt, and

sugar, is so soft that it is almost like a batter. He dredges the tabletop with flour, then scoops mounds of this dough on to it, tossing it through the flour to coat the outside and round it gently. Then he tucks each piece into the wooden frame, two across by four down. Each piece gently flows as Michael shapes the other pieces, and by the time the tray is filled they just barely touch one another.

Then the tray goes into a hot oven for a short bake, where the loaves rise and fill the corners of the frame. This method produces a loaf and crumb superior to that of the usual dough mixed tightly simply to produce a taut clover shape. He works quickly, as the soda reacts as soon as the buttermilk is mixed with it, and my camera struggles to catch his hands as they speed through the shaping.

That evening, William takes me out to drink Guinness in an old drinking house down on the Hook Head peninsula. The loud singing can be heard from the yard outside, and in the smoky warmth from the peat-fuelled fire, we hear songs lamenting love lost, and hard-fought ancient battles against the English, which still bring sadness to the men sat there.

There is a sweet friendliness from the people around me, who are quick to be personal and familiar. I ask William if this is usual. "It's a community built on people helping one another. If someone's car breaks down outside our house, in a way we are really pleased because then, by helping them, we have built up a little bit of credit. So that when we find we need help, they'll be there."

Walnut bread

When making a loaf incorporating nuts or other expensive flavourings, it was once thought sufficient to simply throw scant handfuls of one additional ingredient into the house dough. Not many bakers do that any more. Instead it is usual to layer the flavours through the recipe using different sources. This recipe for walnut bread includes a paste made with walnuts as well as halved walnuts added to the dough. This creates a more complex series of flavours that combine to make a rich, aromatic loaf. This is a bread which I prefer sliced and toasted, spread with a little butter and eaten on its own.

TIP Use good-quality walnuts, ideally the pale sweet ones rather than the darker nuts that seem to taste a little bitter.

Any leftover walnut paste can be eaten as a relish, spread thinly on toast to accompany a slice of mature Cheddar cheese.

FOR THE WALNUT PASTE (makes 100g):

50g walnuts

50g water

2 tbsp honey

20g melted butter, lightly browned

a pinch of fine sea salt

FOR THE DOUGH:

220g water at 20°C (44%)

100g rye leaven (20%)
  (see pages 25–27 and 31)

1¼ tsp fresh yeast, crumbled (1%)

100g walnut paste (20%) (see left)

100g halved walnuts (20%)

350g white flour (70%)

100g rye flour (20%)

50g wholemeal flour (10%)

1½ tsp fine sea salt (2%)

FOR THE WALNUT PASTE Place the walnuts, water, honey, browned butter, and salt in the bowl of a small electric spice or coffee grinder. Grind for a few moments until you have a soft, smooth paste.

FOR THE DOUGH Whisk together the water, rye leaven, and yeast, and then whisk in the walnut paste and fold in the walnut halves. In a second bowl, mix the three flours and the salt, then pour the liquid in with the dry ingredients and combine the dough as evenly as possible, squidging the mixture together with your fingers. Scrape any dough from your fingers into the bowl, cover and leave for 10 minutes.

Rub 1 tsp of corn or olive oil on the work-surface and knead the dough on the oiled surface for 10 seconds, ending with the dough in a smooth, round ball. Clean and dry the bowl, then rub lightly with a tsp of oil. Return the dough to the bowl and leave for a further 10 minutes. Remove the dough, knead once more on the oiled surface, returning the shape of the dough to a smooth, round ball. Place it back in the bowl, cover, and leave for 1 hour in a warm (21–25°C) place.

Take two dry tea-towels and line two 1.5-litre deep bowls with them so that the excess cloth hangs over the edge. Dust the cloths liberally and evenly with flour. Divide the dough into two pieces. Round each piece of dough into a ball and place each ball seam-side-up in the cloth-lined bowls. Cover the dough with the edges of the cloth and leave to rise in a warm place for 2–2½ hours, or until almost doubled in height.

Preheat the oven to 210°C/410°F/gas mark 6½. Carefully upturn the dough out on to a flour-dusted baking sheet, and cut a criss-cross pattern in the top. Bake in the centre of the oven for 50–60 minutes, until the loaf is a good rich brown colour and, when tapped on the bottom, sounds hollow. Leave to cool on a wire rack.

Cobnut loaf with honey and grains

The cobnuts that grow in Kent are a relative of the hazelnut. They first appear covered in a furry green hood that splits at the edges like a medieval trim. Though only occasionally seen in supermarkets, they are easily obtainable by mail order through sites on the internet. At Allens Farm in Sevenoaks, Jill Webb's family picks both the young green nuts from their 100-year old trees, and later the tree-ripened cobnuts, which taste of oak and coconut. The green nuts are available from late August for four weeks, and the ripe cobnuts after that. Even the windfall nuts are collected and stored in barrels to keep the kernels sweet-tasting and moist. I have a handful of last year's windfall crop, which arrived this morning by post, sitting shelled in a bowl, and their texture is still crisp and the flavour perfect. Raw kernels have a beautiful, fresh taste; once baked that changes to the familiar toasted flavour we know from nuts in chocolates and biscuits.

150g strong white flour (30%)

200g soft white flour (40%)

150g strong wholemeal flour (30%)

300g water at 20°C (60%)

1¼ tsp fresh yeast, crumbled (1%)

50g honey (10%)

450g white leaven (90%)
  (see pages 25–27)

185g cobnuts or hazelnuts (shelled weight), toasted and chopped (37%)

200g soaked rye grains (40%)
  (see page 49)

1½ tsp fine sea salt (2%)

50g butter, softened (10%)

Combine the flours lightly and leave to one side. In another bowl, put the water, fresh yeast, and honey. Stir well and leave to sit for 10 minutes.

Add the leaven (broken into small pieces), cobnuts, and soaked grains to the liquid. Stir this liquid into the dry ingredients. Mix the mass together well with your hands, squeezing it through your fingertips. When roughly combined, cover the bowl and leave for 10 minutes.

Tip the dough out on to a lightly floured work-surface, sprinkle over the salt, and dot with the softened butter. Knead the dough gently for 2–3 minutes until everything is combined. Return the dough to the bowl, leave for 30 minutes, then knead once more for a further 2–3 minutes.

Tip the dough out on to a floured work-surface, and give it a turn (see page 21). Leave the dough for a further 30 minutes, then give it one final turn (as above). Cover the dough and leave for 30 minutes. By now the dough will have rested for 1½ hours.

Divide the dough into two pieces, each roughly 875g in weight. On a lightly floured work-surface, roll each piece out into a circle measuring 20cm in diameter. Using a knife, and cutting into the centre from the outside of the loaf, make five incisions 5cm deep to create the shape shown in the picture (right). Stretch each of these segments by pulling them outward slightly. Sit each piece of dough on a flour-dusted tray, then lightly cover them with a cloth and leave to rise for 1 hour.

Preheat the oven to 210°C/410°F/gas mark 6½. Bake in the centre of the oven for 40–50 minutes, until the loaf is a good rich brown in colour and, when tapped on the bottom, sounds hollow. Leave to cool on a wire rack.

Sweet chestnut and hazelnut bread

Chestnut flour is a little difficult to work with, producing a crumbly, dry dough if used on its own. Yet when combined with a large proportion of wheat flour, it gives a subtle flavour and tint to the crumb of the loaf. The sweet, earthy taste can be smoothed by adding fat to the dough, here by using butter and fresh cream, and enhanced by pairing it with hazelnuts. At Locanda Locatelli, we christened this bread *pane di brughiera*, the "*brughiera*" being the land where the pasture meets the woods. It is appropriate for a bread that combines cream and butter with hazelnuts and chestnuts.

FOR THE HAZELNUT CREAM (makes 150g):
50g roasted, skinned hazelnuts
100g single cream

FOR THE DOUGH:
250g strong white flour (61%)
80g strong wholewheat flour (20%)
75g chestnut flour (19%)

1 tsp fine sea salt (2%)
175g water at 20°C (44%)
1½ tsp fresh yeast, crumbled (2%)
150g hazelnut cream (37%)
120g white leaven (30%) (see pages 25–27)
20g unsalted butter, melted (5%)
150g cooked chestnuts, crumbled into pieces (37%)

FOR THE HAZELNUT CREAM Make a paste with the hazelnuts and cream, either in a mortar and pestle or quickly in a blender.

FOR THE DOUGH In a large bowl, combine the flours and salt. In another bowl, whisk the water, yeast, hazelnut cream, and leaven, then tip this into the dry ingredients. Mix this well with your hands until you have a soft, sticky dough, then scrape any dough from your fingers into the bowl, cover and leave for 10 minutes.

Tip the cooled, melted butter over the top of the dough and, working with your fingers, mix it in evenly. Rub 1 tsp of corn or olive oil on the work-surface and knead the dough on the oiled surface for 10 seconds, ending with the dough in a smooth, round ball. Clean and dry the bowl, then rub lightly with a tsp of oil. Leave the dough in the bowl for a further 10 minutes. Knead the dough again on the oiled surface, returning the shape to a smooth, round ball. Leave in the bowl, covered, for 30 minutes in a warm (21–25°C) place.

Place the dough back on the lightly oiled surface. With your fingers, press the dough out into a rough 20x30cm rectangle. Sprinkle the chestnut pieces over the surface of the dough, then roll the dough up tightly so that the chestnuts are trapped inside. Fold the dough roll up by thirds, then tap the dough down to seal the nuts inside. Return the dough to the bowl, cover it with a cloth, and leave for 30 minutes.

Divide the dough into two equal pieces. Shape each into a baton (see page 21). Cover and leave each loaf to rise, seam-side-up, in a basket or tucked in a flour-rubbed cloth for 45 minutes.

Preheat the oven to 210°C/410°F/gas mark 6½. Upturn the loaves on to a baking tray and slash the top with a sharp blade. Lightly spray the surface of each loaf with a mist of water and bake in the centre of the oven for 20 minutes. Reduce the heat to 190°C/375°F/gas mark 5 and bake for a further 45 minutes. The crust will darken considerably due to the butter and cream in the dough. Leave to cool on a wire rack.

Sweet blackcurrant crown

All the ingredients for this loaf were found on Camilla Plum's farm, Fuglebjerggaard (see pages 70–72). The rye flour was freshly milled by her partner, Per Koelster, and the grains were soaked in his home-brewed ale; ripe fruit sagged each willowy branch of the scraggly blackcurrant bushes; there was sweet butter, and the fresh eggs I collected from hens that pecked around the apple orchard. It is a large, beautiful loaf filled with good memories, and a loaf that makes good use of the fruit of late summer. Serve it warm.

TIP The loaf can be made as small or as large as you wish just by changing the number of jam-filled balls you fill it with. It can be easily made in a loaf tin or a round spring-form cake tin. Just don't pack it too tightly, to allow the balls room to rise.

clarified butter to oil the tin

900g sweet yeasted butter dough (100%)
(see page 145)

100g blackcurrant jam (11%)

100g fresh blackcurrants (11%)

100g soft brown sugar (11%)

100g beer-soaked rye grains, cooked
until soft (11%) (see page 49)

Brush the inside of a 20cm diameter *kugelhopf* mould with clarified butter. The loaf will produce a lot of rich syrup, which can cause the bread to stick to the tin, which oiling prevents.

Divide the dough into 18 pieces, each weighing 50g. Lightly flour the palm of your hand, and roll each piece of dough into a ball. Press your thumb into each ball to make a deep indent and put a scant tsp of blackcurrant jam into each one. Pinch the edges together so that the jam is neatly sealed inside the ball of dough. Continue with all the pieces of dough until every one is filled and sealed.

Mix the blackcurrants, brown sugar, and soft rye grains. Place three balls of dough equally spaced apart in the bottom of the buttered mould, then sprinkle with a fifth of the sugar, grain and blackcurrant mix. Fill the spaces in-between with a further three balls, pressing them lightly down and sprinkling them again with a fifth of the sugar, grain and blackcurrant mix. Repeat until you have packed all of the dough balls into the mould together with the sugar mix. Cover the container and leave in a warm place until the dough has almost doubled in height.

Preheat the oven to 200°C/400°F/gas mark 6. Place the tin on a tray and bake in the centre of the oven for 25 minutes. Reduce the heat to 170°C/330°F/ gas mark 3½ and bake for a further 25 minutes. Leave to settle for 2 minutes in the tin, then carefully upturn the bread on to a serving tray, easing it gently out of the mould and being careful to protect your hands from any hot syrup. Serve while hot or warm, with a little custard or cream.

Onion and bay loaf

Bay is a good flavour to partner with onions and milk. It has that soothing aroma that makes a good white sauce taste homely, and in this loaf it adds an unusual fragrance to the crumb. The loaf is perfect toasted to serve with a good smoked kipper, grilled field mushrooms and melted butter.

FOR THE ONIONS: (makes 280g)

280g white onions, diced into 1cm pieces

280g whole milk

3 bay leaves

FOR THE DOUGH:

100g strong wholewheat flour (20%)

400g strong white flour (80%)

1½ tsp fine sea salt (1%)

1¼ tsp fresh yeast, crumbled (1%)

250g milk from the onions (50%)

150g white leaven (30%)
   (see pages 25–27)

280g cooked onions (56%)

Place the chopped onions, milk, and bay leaves in a saucepan and bring to the boil, then remove from the heat and leave to cool for about 30 minutes. Pour through a strainer to separate the onions and bay leaves from the milk. Reserve the milk, for use in the dough.

In a large bowl, combine the flour and salt. In another bowl, whisk the yeast with 250g of the milk in which the onions have been cooked. Beat in the leaven until the mixture is smooth, then finally add the onions and stir. Pour the wet ingredients in with the flour, and stir until you have a soft sticky dough. Scrape any dough from your fingers into the bowl, then cover and leave for 10 minutes.

Rub 1 tsp of corn or olive oil on the work-surface and knead the dough on the oiled surface for 10 seconds, ending with the dough in a smooth, round ball. Clean and dry the bowl, then rub with a tsp of oil. Return the dough to the bowl and leave for a further 10 minutes. Remove the dough and knead once more on the oiled surface, returning the shape of the dough to a smooth, round ball. Place it back in the bowl, cover, and leave for 1 hour in a warm (21–25°C) place.

Line a deep 20cm diameter bowl with a flour-rubbed tea towel. Lightly flour the work-surface and shape the dough into a ball (see page 21). Place the ball of dough seam-side-upwards into the cloth, then cover it with the exposed corners of the tea-towel. Leave the bowl in a warm (21–25°C) place for 1½ hours, or until the loaf has doubled in height.

Preheat the oven to 210°C/410°F/gas mark 6½. Upturn the loaf on to a semolina-dusted baking tray. Spray the upper surface of the dough with a fine mist of water, then place the tray in the centre of the oven and bake for 20 minutes. Reduce the heat to 190°C/375°F/gas mark 5 and bake for a further 30 minutes, until the loaf is a good dark brown colour. Leave to cool on a wire rack.

Almond-milk loaf

250g plain white flour (50%)

250g strong white flour (50%)

1½ tsp fine sea salt (2%)

150g skinned almonds (30%)

20g caster sugar (4%)

325g water at 20°C (65%)

2 tsp fresh yeast, crumbled (2%)

Eliza Acton, in her *English Bread Book*, describes an almond bread recipe entitled "Turkish Bread". Though I can't find a mention of such a loaf in any books on Turkish cuisine, they may have existed: Victorian England had such a fascination with the architecture and stories of the Levant that the desire to attribute recipes to these places must have been alluring. This recipe takes a type of nut milk sold in Italy – a marzipan that is mixed with water to make a iced summertime drink – and uses it as the liquid to moisten the dough. Though it is not a sweet dough, the almonds increase the protein slightly and make it a good, filling loaf.

TIP For the bread in the photograph, I've used a Pullman tin. This is a bread-baking tin with a lid that slides over the top, which you can buy at specialist kitchenware stores or by mail order.

Mix the plain and strong flours with the salt in a large bowl. Using a mortar and pestle, or a blender, grind the almonds to a creamy paste with the sugar and 100g of the water, then beat in the remaining water and the yeast. Stir this liquid in with the dry ingredients and mix it all together until you have a soft, sticky dough. Scrape any dough from your fingers into the bowl, then cover and leave for 10 minutes.

Rub 1 tsp of corn or olive oil on the work-surface and knead the dough on the oiled surface for 10 seconds, ending with the dough in a smooth, round ball. Clean and dry the bowl, then rub lightly with a tsp of oil. Return the dough to the bowl and leave for a further 10 minutes. Remove the dough, knead once more on the oiled surface, returning the shape of the dough to a smooth, round ball. Place it back in the bowl, cover, and leave for 1 hour in a warm (21–25°C) place.

Oil and flour a deep loaf tin (10 x 18cm). Lightly flour the work-surface and shape the dough into a baton (see page 21). This time, however, tap the ends in before rolling it back and forth to form a smooth cylinder the same length as the tin. Drop the dough seam-side-upwards into the tin, and leave to rise for 1½ hours or until doubled in height. If you're using a Pullman tin, add the greased lid at this point.

Preheat the oven to 210°C/410°F/gas mark 6½. For an open top loaf, lightly dust the dough surface with flour. For a closed Pullman loaf, just check that the dough nearly touches the lid. Bake in the centre of the oven for 25 minutes, then reduce the heat to 190°C/375°F/gas mark 5 and bake for a further 20 minutes, until the loaf is a good golden-brown. Leave to cool on a wire rack.

White potato stottie cake

The stottie cake is the flatbread from the city of heroes, Newcastle upon Tyne. Although almost unknown outside its home region, we should recognize it as one of the great breads of Europe. It is a thin disc of good white dough that is baked on hot stones in the oven before being flipped and baked on the other side. Ian Gregg's eponymous bakery used to have an oven in the old Grainger market, just up from the tripe stall, and here the bakers would flip stotties during the day. At its best, the stottie is like a large perfect white muffin (not the cake sort), tinged brown on both sides with a very soft tender crumb. As cooked potatoes would have been added to the dough on occasion, I've included them in this recipe to add heartiness to a simple loaf. Rather than attempting to flip these, I find it best to lay a second tray on top of the unbaked stotties, weighted down by something heavy and ovenproof to hold the tray in place during baking.

500g strong white flour (100%)

1½ tsp fine sea salt (2%)

300g water at 20°C (60%)

300g cooked potato, mashed (60%)

2 tsp fresh yeast, crumbled (2%)

In a large bowl, mix the flour with the salt. In another bowl, whisk the water with the mashed potato and yeast, then pour this in with the dry ingredients. Stir the mixture together with your hands until you have a soft, sticky dough.

Rub 1 tsp of corn or olive oil on the work-surface and knead the dough on the oiled surface for 10 seconds, ending with the dough in a smooth, round ball. Clean and dry the bowl, then rub lightly with a tsp of oil. Return the dough to the bowl and leave for a further 10 minutes. Remove the dough, knead once more on the oiled surface, returning the shape of the dough to a smooth round ball. Place it back in the bowl, cover, and leave for 1 hour in a warm (21–25°C) place.

Divide the dough into four equal pieces, each roughly 280g in weight. On a lightly floured surface roll each piece into a round disc measuring 15cm in diameter. Lay each disc on a floured tray. Cover with a cloth and leave to rise for 45 minutes, or until almost doubled in height.

Preheat the oven to 210°C/410°F/gas mark 6½. Uncover the unbaked stotties and lightly sift flour evenly over the upper surface of each loaf. Place a clean baking tray directly on top of the dough, so it is sandwiched between two sheets of metal, and bake in the centre of the oven for 30 minutes. Carefully lift off the upper tray and, using a spatula, transfer the baked stotties to a wire rack. When cool, wrap well to stop them from drying out.

Layered apple and custard loaf

Thick custard, brown sugar, and good eating apples are layered between discs of buttery dough, then baked to form one loaf. This is perhaps not the most delicate of breads but, like rice pudding or plum *clafoutis*, it is good, hearty stodge – perfect after an energetic day in the field or garden; the sort of fruit-bread children seem to understand very well.

450g sweet yeasted butter dough)
  (see page 145)
700g pastry custard (see page 187)

5 good eating apples
100g soft brown sugar

Line the base and sides of a 25cm springform cake tin with non-stick baking paper (or well buttered brown paper). Peel and core the apples and cut into slices.

Divide the dough into three pieces, each weighing roughly 150g. On a flour-dusted work-surface roll each piece of dough out into a disc 25cm in diameter (the same size as the cake tin). Place one in the bottom on the tin, then spread a third of the custard over the surface. Cover the custard with a third of the apples, then sprinkle with a third of the sugar. Repeat with the other pieces of dough, the remaining custard, apples, and sugar. Sprinkle the upper surface of the unbaked loaf with the last of the sugar, and leave in a warm (21–25°C) place to prove for 1½ hours.

Preheat the oven to 200°C/400°F/gas mark 6. Bake on a rack in the centre of the oven for 10 minutes. Reduce the heat to 170°C/330°F/gas mark 3½ and bake for a further 35 minutes, covering the top of the cake at the end if it gets too brown. Leave in the tin to cool, and serve when warm.

Herbs, spices, & fragrances

In Yaroslava Kharuk's kitchen in the Ukrainian city of Ivano-Frankivsk, the garden herbs were spread out over trays lined with white cloth and left to dry slowly in the warmth. It was the end of autumn. The trees outside were stripped bare by the wind and the soil had already begun to harden in the cold. But here in the heat of kitchen, the last remaining edible leaves were being stored to ensure that some of that flavour could be added to winter foods.

For flavouring, we take the bright-tasting ingredients of one season and apply them to another less palatable food, modifying and tempering the flavour so that it has the hint of something familiar and appealing. Spices and herbs, when combined with a dominant helping of sugar or salt, nudge foods towards either sweet or savoury: sweet cinnamon and apple, for example, or savoury mustard and apple.

What these additional flavours and aromas do is offer us a choice, multiplying the possible dishes that can be created from a small garden and extending the number of breads that can be baked from a single grain. Sometimes herbs and spices add a playful novelty to a loaf's taste, or establish its tradition, or act solely as a marker to advise a customer or assistant in a bakery what type of loaf it is.

There are great dishes and breads that combine many spices, for example the Bavarian breads that use a complex mixture of fennel, caraway, anise and dill, and the many different spice mixtures for gingerbread. But don't overlook the value of a herb, spice, vegetable or strongly scented oil. Coriander alone can make a notable rye bread by imparting a fragrant bitter taste, a little like the white pith of an orange, to a dark loaf.

Black pepper pancakes

Thin, crisp-edged pancakes or crêpes are, like a loaf at the table, an elegant way of extending more expensive ingredients. Wrapped around spinach and ricotta, or braised endive and bacon, they turn the fillings into simple, pleasurable meals.

2 medium eggs (96%)

300g milk at 20°C (240%)

125g plain flour (100%)

½ tsp fine sea salt (2%)

¾ tsp freshly ground black pepper (3%)

25g unsalted butter, melted (20%)

In a bowl or jug, beat the eggs with the milk. Sift the flour and whisk this into the liquid. Stir in the salt and black pepper, then beat in the melted butter. Cover the bowl and refrigerate for 2 hours.

Preheat a non-stick frying pan, and add 1 tsp of olive oil, lard or butter, heating until it is almost smoking hot. Remove the pan from the heat and rub any excess oil from the surface using a few sheets of scrunched-up kitchen towel.

Ladle 2–3 tbsp batter into the centre of the pan, turning it so the batter spreads thinly. Return to the heat and cook for 2–3 minutes, until the edges are crisp and brown and the surface is broken with air bubbles that go through to the base of the pan. With a spatula, loosen the pancake from the frying pan and flip over. Cook for another minute, or until both sides are brown. Sometimes the first pancake sticks a little, but if it does simply rub off any stuck bits and rub oil once more on to the surface.

Remove the pancake from the pan, place on a plate, and cover with a cloth while you cook the remaining pancakes.

Sweet saffron bread

This bread uses what bakers call a "sponge": equal quantities of flour and liquid mixed with a small amount of yeast. If you look at the procedure to make a naturally leavened bread (see page 28), this is similar but mightily accelerated.

FOR THE SPONGE:

100g milk at 20°C

¾ tsp fresh yeast, crumbled

100g plain flour

FOR THE DOUGH:

12 threads saffron (0.5%)

¾ tbsp boiling water (24%)

250g strong white flour (100%)

25g caster sugar (10%)

scant ½ tsp fine sea salt (1%)

30g unsalted butter, softened (12%)

150g milk at 20°C (60%)

the sponge (80%)

100g currants (40%)

cornmeal for dusting the tray

egg wash for glazing (see page 187)

FOR THE   In a bowl, beat together the milk, yeast, and flour until smooth. Cover and leave in a warm (25°C) place for 1 hour, until the mixture is bubbling and smells yeasty.

FOR THE   Cover the saffron with the boiling water and leave for 10 minutes to infuse.

In a large bowl, combine the flour with the sugar and salt. Break the butter into small pieces, then rub this through the flour until it disappears and no lumps remain. In another bowl or jug, whisk the milk with the saffron water, then stir this in with the sponge. Keep stirring until the mixture has evenly combined, then mix in the currants. Pour this liquid in with the flour and stir until you have a soft, sticky dough. Scrape any dough from your fingers into the bowl, cover and leave for 10 minutes.

Rub 1 tsp of corn or olive oil on the work-surface and knead the dough on the oiled surface for 10 seconds, ending with it in a smooth, round ball. Clean and dry the bowl, then rub lightly with a tsp of oil. Return the dough to the bowl and leave for a further 10 minutes. Remove the dough and knead once more on the oiled surface, returning the shape of the dough to a smooth round ball. Place it back in the bowl, cover, and leave for 1 hour in a warm (21–25°C) place.

Lightly dust the work-surface and shape the dough into a baton (see page 21). Cover with a cloth and leave for 10 minutes for the dough to soften and relax. Roll the dough out using your floured hands until you have a piece measuring 50cm long. Spiral each end, in opposite directions, until you have an elaborate "S"-shape. Sprinkle a large 30x40cm tray with cornmeal, then place the dough in the centre of the tray. Cover lightly with a cloth and leave for 1 hour, or until almost doubled in height.

Preheat the oven to 210°C/410°F/gas mark 6½. Uncover the loaf and brush the surface gently and lightly with egg wash. Bake in the centre of the oven for 30 minutes, then reduce the heat to 190°C/375°F/gas mark 5 and bake for a further 15–20 minutes, until the loaf is a good brown colour, feels light in weight, and sounds hollow when tapped on the base. Leave to cool on a wire rack.

Parsley potato cakes

This is a potato scone, fried in a dry pan over a gentle heat. If you're feeling nimble you could bake it, as it would have traditionally been, on a griddle or girdle. But the handle on the frying pan makes it easier to flip. Non-stick pans make this task easy, but if you don't have one then use a heavy-bottomed iron frying pan that has been oiled and heated to a high temperature, then allowed to cool before using. This makes food less likely to stick. Serve like bubble and squeak for a late big breakfast, together with bacon, eggs and grilled large field mushrooms.

125g plain white flour (100%)

½ tsp bicarbonate of soda (2%)

½ tsp fine sea salt (2%)

60g unsalted butter, softened (48%)

250g potato, cooked and mashed (200%)

1 medium egg (48%)

100g milk at 20°C (80%)

2 tbsp fresh chopped parsley (4%)

dripping or oil

In a large bowl, combine the flour with the soda and salt. Break the butter into small pieces and rub it into the flour mixture until no lumps remain. In another bowl, whisk the mashed potato with the egg, then beat in the milk and parsley. Pour this in with the dry ingredients and stir until you have an evenly combined, soft and sticky dough.

Take a large frying pan, ideally one with a close-fitting lid. Melt 1 tbsp of dripping (or sunflower oil) in the pan, then swirl the pan to coat the base evenly. Place this over a heat-diffusing plate on a low heat, and scrape the dough into the pan. Quickly pat the surface smooth with a spatula, then leave to cook over a gentle heat for 4–5 minutes, preferably with a lid on. As you need to cook the flour out, it is vital to keep the heat low and extend the cooking time. Aim for a crisp, slightly brown base to the cake after about 5 minutes.

Liberally oil a large dinner plate. Place this over the top of the frying pan then, using a thick cloth, flip the pan over so that the cake falls down on to the plate. Slide the upturned cake back into the pan, return to the heat, and cook for a further 4–5 minutes.

To serve, flip the cake out on to the oiled plate and cut into wedges, or simply put crisp bacon, grilled mushrooms, and tomatoes on the top and serve it straight out of the pan – but that might be too piggy!

Chelsea buns

The traditional Chelsea bun has a slight lemon flavour, and the dough would be dusted with nutmeg before rolling. By the early 20th-century, cinnamon became the preferred spice. I've used nutmeg, as I prefer its taste combined with lemon in the bun. Lard would have been used for rolling, but I prefer butter, or at least half butter and half lard.

FOR THE FILLING:

50g soft brown sugar

50g caster sugar

50g unsalted butter, softened

zest of ¼ lemon

¼ tsp freshly grated nutmeg

100g currants

TO SERVE:

melted butter for greasing the tin

caster sugar for dredging

FOR THE DOUGH:

150g plain white flour (33%)

300g strong white flour (67%)

1 tsp fine sea salt (2%)

100g milk at 20°C (22%)

100g water at 20°C (22%)

2 medium eggs (27%)

50g golden syrup (11%)

2 tsp fresh yeast, crumbled (3%)

FOR THE FILLING Combine all the ingredients apart from the currants until you have a soft paste. Leave this in a warm (21–25°C) place while you make the dough.

FOR THE DOUGH In a large bowl, combine the two flours with the salt. In another bowl or jug, place the milk, water, eggs, golden syrup, and fresh yeast. Whisk until smooth. Pour the liquid in with the dry ingredients and stir with your hands until you have a soft, sticky dough. Scrape any dough from your fingers into the bowl, cover and leave for 10 minutes.

Rub 1 tsp of corn or olive oil on the work-surface and knead the dough on the oiled surface for 10 seconds, ending with the dough in a smooth, round ball. Clean and dry the bowl, then rub lightly with a tsp of oil. Return the dough to the bowl and leave for a further 10 minutes. Knead the dough once more on the oiled surface, returning it to a smooth, round ball. Place it back in the bowl, cover, and leave for 1 hour in a warm (21–25°C) place.

Line a 30cm square cake tin with non-stick baking parchment on the base and brush the paper and sides with melted butter. Lightly dust the work-surface with flour and roll the dough out into a 35cm square. Crumble the filling over the dough and press it down into the surface, then scatter the currants evenly across the dough. Roll the dough up tightly from one end. Cut the dough into nine equal pieces, then place these (three across by three down) in the tin. Cover the tin with a cloth and leave to rise for 1 hour.

Preheat the oven to 210°C/410°F/gas mark 6½. Uncover the tin and dredge the surface of the dough with caster sugar. Bake in the centre of the oven for 30 minutes, then reduce the heat to 190°C/375°F/gas mark 5 and bake for a further 15–20 minutes, until the buns are a good brown colour on top. Leave to cool on a wire rack for 10 minutes. Brush the top of the buns with sugar glaze (see page 188) and serve warm.

Rye with coriander

FOR THE SPONGE:

150g rye leaven

   (see pages 25–27 and 31)

450g water at 20°C

½ tsp fresh yeast, crumbled

10g bran

50g ground malted barley or rye

   (see page 38–39)

FOR THE DOUGH:

2 tsp coriander seeds (2%)

250g light rye flour (62.5%)

150g strong white flour (37.5%)

1 tsp fine sea salt (2%)

the sponge (165%)

This dark bread is reminiscent of the bread served in small, traditional cafeterias in Russia and the Ukraine, and it is an acquired taste. It has a hefty dose of freshly ground coriander seed worked into the dough, giving the crumb a slight bitterness, like the white pith of an orange. It offsets the sweetness of malt and is a traditional favouring for some old ales and beers.

FOR THE SPONGE In a bowl, beat together the rye leaven, water, yeast, bran, and malt until you have a smooth paste. Cover and leave for 1½ hours, or until bubbly and fermenting.

FOR THE DOUGH In a large bowl, combine the coriander seeds, rye and white flours, and salt. Toss with your fingers until lightly combined, then mix in the sponge liquid, squeezing the mixture through your fingertips until evenly combined. Scrape any dough from your fingers into the bowl, cover and leave for 10 minutes.

Rub 1 tsp of corn or olive oil on the work-surface and knead the dough on the oiled surface for 10 seconds, ending with a smooth, round ball. Clean and dry the bowl, then rub lightly with a tsp of oil. Return the dough to the bowl, cover and leave for a further 10 minutes. Remove the dough and knead once more on the oiled surface, returning the shape of the dough to a smooth, round ball. Place it back in the bowl, cover, and leave for 1 hour in a warm (21–25°C) place.

Oil and flour a 20x10cm oblong loaf tin. Lightly dust the work-surface with flour and shape the dough into a baton (see page 21). Drop the baton into the tin, and press it down with your knuckles until it sits evenly inside. Cover the tin lightly with a cloth and leave in a warm (21–25°C) place for ¾ hour, or until risen by a third and just about over the top of the tin.

Preheat the oven to 210°C/410°F/gas mark 6½. Uncover the loaf and, using a sharp blade, slash down the middle of the top of the loaf. Mist the upper surface of the dough lightly with water. Bake in the centre of the oven for 30 minutes, then reduce the heat to 190°C/375°F/gas mark 5 and bake for a further 15–20 minutes, until the loaf is a good brown colour, feels light in weight, and sounds hollow when tapped on the base. Leave to cool on a wire rack for 10 minutes, then remove the loaf from the tin and leave it to cool upright on a wire rack.

Orange and almond cake

This is a dessert bread. The sweet little cakes are served with cream and fruit, or cut into wedges and spread with unsalted butter and lemon curd. Or you could use the dough as a soft top over a dish of poached apricots, baking them both until the crust is crisp and golden and the apricots bubbling hot.

TIP As an alternative to making four round cakes, you can simply pat the dough out on to a paper-lined tray in one piece, dredge it with sugar and bake, then cut into squares or fingers while still warm.

100g blanched and peeled almonds, ground (66%)

150g plain flour (100%)

80g caster sugar (53%)

1 tsp baking powder (2%)

50g unsalted butter, softened (33%)

50g double cream (33%)

60g whole milk at 20°C (40%)

zest of 1 orange (2%)

slivered almonds

caster sugar for dredging

Preheat the oven to 220°C/425°F/gas mark 7. Line a 40x30cm tray with non-stick baking parchment.

In a large bowl, combine the ground almonds, flour, sugar, and baking powder. Toss with your fingers until evenly combined, then break the butter into small pieces and rub this through the flour until the mixture resembles fine breadcrumbs.

In a jug or another bowl, beat the cream with the milk and orange zest. Stir this in with the dry ingredients until you have a soft smooth paste.

Scrape the dough out on to a plate and divide into four even pieces. Wet your fingers and shape each piece into a ball, then squash it flat on the paper-lined tray so that it sits 2cm high by about 8cm in diameter. Strew a few slivers of almond on top of each cake, and dredge heavily with the additional caster sugar.

Bake in the centre of the oven for 18–20 minutes, or until risen and golden brown on top. Remove from the oven and, after a few moments, transfer the cakes to a wire cooling rack. When warm, serve with a little softly whipped cream and soft fruit.

131

Lemon barley cob

This is a hearty loaf, though its name might suggest a delicate appearance. It is sprinkled with coarse flakes of sea salt before baking, which stick out like prickles on the tan-brown crust. Barley benefits from a little acidity and the grated zest of lemon, plus the juice in the dough, picks the flavour up and lends it a gentle rye-like tang. Serve this as a sandwich bread, filled with oily, bright things such as grilled peppers and soft olive paste, together with cheese and ham. A handful of soft lamb's lettuce between the slices is the best finish.

100g barley flour (40%)
150g strong white flour (60%)
¾ tsp fine sea salt (2%)
150g white leaven (60%)
  (see pages 25–27)
150g water at 20°C (60%)

1 tbsp lemon juice (6%)
zest of 1 lemon (2%)
30g honey (12%)
¾ tsp fresh yeast, crumbled (1%)
coarse sea salt for sprinkling

In a large bowl, combine the barley and strong white flours with the salt. In another bowl or jug, whisk together the leaven, water, lemon juice and zest, honey, and yeast until smooth and combined. Stir this liquid in with the dry ingredients and mix until you have an evenly-combined, soft and sticky dough. Scrape any dough from your fingers into the bowl, cover and leave for 10 minutes.

Rub 1 tsp of corn or olive oil on the work-surface and knead the dough on the oiled surface for 10 seconds, ending with a smooth, round ball. Clean and dry the bowl, then rub lightly with a tsp of oil. Return the dough to the bowl and leave for a further 10 minutes. Knead the dough once more on the oiled surface, returning the shape of the dough to a smooth, round ball. Place it back in the bowl, cover and leave for 1 hour in a warm (21–25°C) place.

Lightly dust the work-surface and shape the dough into a baton (see page 21). Rub flour into a tea-towel (or use a linen-lined proving basket) and place the dough inside, seam-side-up. Wrap the dough up snugly in the cloth, and leave to rise for 1½ hours, or until almost doubled in height.

Preheat the oven to 210°C/410°F/gas mark 6½. Upturn the loaf on to a flour- or semolina-dusted tray, spray (or brush) the upper surface with water, then sprinkle the surface with flaked crystal sea salt. Using a sharp blade, slash the loaf along the length. Bake in the centre of the oven for 30 minutes, then reduce the heat to 190°C/375°F/gas mark 5 and bake for a further 15–20 minutes, until the loaf is a good brown colour, feels light in weight, and sounds hollow when tapped on the base. Leave to cool on a wire rack.

White thyme bread

Jack Lang, a passionate home baker in Cambridge, has a wood-fired oven in his garden, sitting under the apple trees like an old, miniature house, with a pointed roof covered in different varieties of thyme. In summer, small flowers appear dotted among the leaves, their roots tickled by the insulated warmth of the oven dome below. Thyme is an excellent herb to mix into an olive oil dough as the oil helps spread the flavour from the herb through every slice. For this bread I use picholine olives, which have a crisp, rather than soft, texture, and a sweet, nutty taste. Pit these by hand, pressing them firmly down on to the work-surface to split them in two, then picking out the stone with your fingers. Tricky, I know, but the flavour is worth the effort.

350g strong white flour (100%)

1 tsp fine sea salt (2%)

150g water at 20°C (43%)

150g white leaven (43%)
  (see pages 25–27)

½ tsp fresh yeast, crumbled (1%)

25g extra virgin olive oil (7%)

100g pitted green olives (29%)

1 tsp chopped fresh thyme (1.5%)

polenta or cornmeal for dusting

In a large bowl, combine the flour with the salt, tossing it together with your fingers. In another bowl, whisk together the water, leaven, yeast, 25g olive oil, the olives, and thyme. Pour this liquid in with the flour, then stir with your hands until you have a soft, sticky dough. Scrape any dough from your fingers into the bowl, cover and leave for 10 minutes.

Rub a good tsp of olive oil on to a clean work-surface and lightly knead the dough on the oiled surface for 10 seconds. Return the dough to the bowl and leave for 10 minutes. Repeat this brief kneading, using a little more oil if necessary, then return the dough to the bowl and leave for a further 10 minutes. Knead the dough once more on the oiled surface, return to the bowl and leave for another 10 minutes.

Generously oil a lipped tray. Place the dough seam-side-down on the oiled tray and pat it out into a rectangle, then fold it in by thirds each way. Flip the dough over so that the seam side faces down. Place the cloth back over the dough and leave for 1 hour in a warm (21–25°C) place. Stretch the dough, fold as before, and leave again for an hour. Repeat this stretching and folding once more and leave to rise again for an hour. Each time you gently stretch and fold the dough, try to keep as much air in it as you can and avoid flattening it. It is important that the temperature of the dough does not rise above 21–25°C; it should always feel cool to the touch. When the dough is ready, a cut into the centre should reveal a network of holes.

Lightly oil a 30x20cm baking tray, and sprinkle the surface lightly with polenta. Flip the dough out on to the centre of the tray, then dimple the surface with your fingertips to slightly flatten it. Sprinkle the upper surface of the dough with polenta too, then loosely cover the dough with a cloth and leave for 30–45 minutes, ideally in a warmer place near the oven at 25–28°C.

Preheat the oven to 220°C/425°F/gas mark 7. Uncover the dough and bake in the centre of the oven for 40 minutes, or until the upper surface is a good golden brown. Using a spatula, ease the bread from the tray and leave it to cool on a wire rack.

Sweden

There is an impressive, modern artisan baking culture in Sweden, and much of it stems from the work and influence of one man: Jan Hedh. Hedh is an accomplished craftsman and his bakery, near the coastal town of Ystad, has produced many of the region's talented bakers. His approach to bread-making – to respect the provenance of ingredients and to maintain traditional Swedish recipes and techniques – has earned him the deep respect, in turn, of the "new guard" bakers in Stockholm. He is a gentle giant of a man, deeply knowledgeable and experienced, and we drank mightily into the night as we talked about rye breads, baking, and life.

Early the following morning, we make our way to Hedh's bakery, Olof Viktors, in Glemmingebro. Standing beside a patch of woodland is a traditional large, square, white-brick building with gates on one side leading to a courtyard in the centre. At one end stands the bakery, with a modern wood-fired oven, designed by Hedh, which is fuelled by timber from the forest. His young team had started early this morning. The day before, he had baked a dozen saffron loaves, curled and twisted and egg glazed before baking. They look like bronze artefacts, somewhat medieval and regal.

By the door, hanging on a wooden rod, are discs of *knäckebröd*, Swedish rye crisp bread that dry as they hang in the warm air. Crisp breads traditionally kept the harvested grain edible through the winter months and were hung up to keep them away from vermin. Though now we think of crisp breads as little oblongs wrapped in paper, with the bite and crunch of potato crisps, they were once far sturdier – and they still are today, when made by small artisan bakers in Sweden.

Swedish food writer Dag Hermelin suggested I go to visit Roslagsbröd, where the best *knäckebröd* in Sweden is made. The bakery is in a town called Gimo, north of Stockholm, and I reckoned on a few hours travelling time. The trip involved a train, then a bus, then a car – a combination that seemed sure to swallow the hours. But here technology lives up to its promise and all the connections, and the time taken to make them (even footsteps along the snow-covered bus depot), are measured and accounted for. The winter sun stays low during the day and skates across the horizon on a pink-hued path; the trip seemed to hover in a twilight moment, like those ever-lasting sunsets you view from the window of a jet plane.

LEFT, FROM TOP: Johan Sörbergs; Leif Torstensson; Jonas Adolffson; Dag Hermelin; Jan Hedh. ABOVE, FROM TOP: *knäckebröd*; Johan Sörbergs breaking crisp bread; Sörbergs' rye flatbreads; salty sweet rye; OPPOSITE, CLOCKWISE FROM TOP LEFT: Chef Östen Brolin and baker Richard Bingham at Vete Katten in Stockholm; *knäckebröd* at Roslagsbröd; the window at Riddarbageriet; spiced rye flatbread; Jan Hedh's wheaten loaf; soft anise and fennel *oälkaka*; saffron crown; sweet saffron pastry; soft rye bread; apple Danish; *knäckebröd* at Hedh's bakery; baker at Riddarbageriet; sky in Gimo; caraway crispbread at Riddarbageriet; CENTRE: Johan Sörbergs and bakers at Riddarbageriet; Christmas wheat *knäckebröd* at Roslagsbröd.

The bakery stands in a small warehouse, which was built in 1922 by B. E. Sandstrom and his family and then renovated in 1996 after it was brought by Robert Saberski, who also reinstated the former baker, Leif Torstensson.

The bakery is mechanised, but only in the sense that a farmer with a plough is mechanised. Most of the machinery and the large oven date from its opening in the 1920s. A pinkish daylight streams in through large frosted windows around two sides; the walls are lined with glazed white oblong tiles coated with a dusting of rye flour.

The large, free-spinning bowl of a slow dough-mixer judders around as its curved wishbone blade flips the dough over and over. This mixture of rye, leaven, salt and water is sloppy, like thick, green-grey porridge, and is scooped with a spade by baker Tobbe Engberg into a strange, aging Heath Robinson contraption (minus the buzzers and whistles) painted buttercup yellow. There, knobbly rollers run back and forth over the dough as it is scraped over a cloth belt. A continual dredging of coarse rye flour rains down to contain the stickiness, and a wheel rolls a round stamp across to make the distinctive gramophone record shape with a hole in the middle.

And there, at the end, with a flat shovel, is Leif, who scoops the flatbreads on to a dozen thin, wooden planks that sit 10cm above each other on a trolley. These are wheeled into a warm, damp room, where they puff up from 3mm thick to double that. Then Leif scoops them deftly on to the wire grid of the oven and they travel through to be almost grilled in the intense heat. As the rye lacks the sugars that colour wheaten breads, it takes a fierce heat to tinge the crust brown. They sit above the oven, in a practice dating back centuries, to crisp and dry.

Johan Sörbergs, a former student of Jan Hedh's, has set up a small bakery in the centre of Stockholm that is unabashedly young, feisty, loud, and innovative – qualities rarely found in bakeries within traditional communities. At Riddarbageriet, even the windows that expose the workings to the street have a brazen appearance. Yet the chunks of sweet gingerbread, the paper-thin *knäckebröd* topped with local seeds and berries, and the little saffron buns curled into a snake-like "S" shape, all resolutely stem from heartfelt respect for Swedish culture. Johan is simply the provocateur that pushes it forward.

Johan and I talk about burnt-top breads, the now almost forbidden practice. Today burnt crusts are viewed as deadly at worst, and certainly a waste. But without the penetrating effect of the browning or charring, the crumb flavour is thin and wanting. "It is always a battle", says Johan. "I would prefer to bake darker, like all bakers, but we struggle with the customer's ever-heightened anxiety. Has there ever been a 'burnt bread' related illness?"

By 8am a queue of a dozen customers is standing out into the street, even though the temperature dips well below zero. Inside the few tables are filled with people chatting and feasting on sweet freshly-baked morning breads and hot coffee. This is modern baking, a re-establishment of the relationship between the customer and the craftsperson based on respect and trust. "Customers come in and ask me what to buy, what's good today," says Johan, "and I think it's because they believe that I'll tell them the truth. And you know what? I would be honest every time."

"Today burnt crusts are viewed as deadly at worst... But without the penetrating effect of the browning and charring, the crumb flavour is thin."

Mustard and maize rolls

These are perfect spread with butter and wedged with a slice of good fatty ham and small sprigs of crisp watercress.

FOR THE DOUGH:

200g strong white flour (80%)

50g fine maize flour (20%)

¾ tsp fine sea salt (2%)

1 tsp English mustard powder (2%)

100g white leaven (40%)
   (see pages 25–7)

125g water at 20°C (50%)

¾ tsp fresh yeast, crumbled (1%)

FOR THE MUSTARD WASH:

1 tsp English mustard powder

2 tsp water

1 tbsp olive oil

In a large bowl, combine the strong white and maize flours with the salt and mustard powder. In another bowl or jug, whisk the leaven with the water and yeast. Pour the liquid in with the dry ingredients and stir well until you have a soft, sticky dough. Scrape any dough from your fingers into the bowl, cover, and leave for 10 minutes.

Rub 1 tsp of corn or olive oil on the work-surface and knead the dough on the oiled surface for 10 seconds, ending with a smooth, round ball. Clean and dry the bowl, then rub lightly with 1 tsp of oil. Return the dough to the bowl and leave for a further 10 minutes. Remove the dough and knead on the oiled surface for 10 seconds, returning the shape of the dough to a smooth, round ball. Place it back in the bowl, cover, and leave for 1 hour in a warm (21–25°C) place.

Divide the dough into eight pieces, each weighing approximately 60g. Round each piece tightly into a ball, and then sit it on a lightly floured work-surface, covered with a cloth. Leave to rise for 45 minutes.

Mix together the ingredients for the mustard wash in a small ramekin.

Preheat the oven to 210°C/410°F/gas mark 6½. Lightly dust a 40x30cm tray with maize flour. With the handle of a wooden spoon, press down into each ball of dough until there is only a membrane left between the two halves, then brush along the indent with a little of the mustard wash. Press the two halves back together, then place the roll on the tray. Repeat with the remaining dough balls.

Spray a fine mist of water on top of the unbaked rolls. Bake for 20 minutes, then reduce the heat to 190°C/375°F/gas mark 5 and bake for a further 15–20 minutes, until the rolls are a good golden brown. Transfer the rolls on to a wire rack to cool.

Honey and ginger wafers

Gingerbread-making has almost become a lost art. There were once associations of gingerbread-makers, who perfected this quite separate skill. One book I have lists 30 different spice mixtures, suggesting that each baker saw the combination of imported spices as his signature. These little wafers are often decorated with something more complicated than the mark of a fork that I've made here. But there is something appealing – almost Celtic – about this cross pattern, and I like it. Store the gingerbread in an airtight box for a few days with half an apple to keep them soft and moist.

FOR THE SPICE MIX:

1 tsp whole coriander seeds

1 tsp ground cinnamon

¼ tsp grated nutmeg

¼ tsp whole black peppercorns

1 tsp ground ginger

2 cardamom pods

¼ tsp fennel seeds

FOR THE DOUGH:

250g runny honey (83%)

150g unsalted butter (50%)

2 tbsp double cream (10%)

150g plain white flour (50%)

150g light rye flour (50%)

1 tsp bicarbonate of soda (1.5%)

100g soft brown sugar (33%)

spice mix (1.5%)

FOR THE GLAZE:

1 medium egg plus 1 egg yolk

1 tbsp water

¼ tsp fine sea salt

FOR THE SPICE MIX Pound the spice ingredients together in a mortar and pestle (or an electric spice grinder) until fine.

FOR THE DOUGH In a saucepan, heat the honey with the butter over a low heat until the butter has melted. Stir and leave to cool until warm, then stir in the double cream.

In a large bowl, combine the plain white and rye flours with the soda and soft brown sugar. Add the spice mix and toss with your fingers. Pour the warm honey, butter, and cream mixture in with the dry ingredients and stir until you have a smooth dough. Cover with a damp cloth, and leave it to sit for 20 minutes for the dough to soften, or wrap well and leave at room temperature (21°C) overnight.

Preheat the oven to 210°C/410°F/gas mark 6½. Lightly dust the work-surface with flour and place the dough on top of it. Using a rolling pin, roll out the dough to a thickness of 5mm. Using an 8cm round cutter, cut rounds of dough and place them on a 30 x 40cm tray lined with non-stick baking parchment. You will need to bake these wafers in batches.

FOR THE GLAZE Whisk the egg, yolk, water, and salt together, then brush the surface of each gingerbread with this egg wash. Use the prongs of a fork to make a cross mark in the surface of each wafer.

Bake in the centre of the oven for 15 minutes, or until the egg wash on the surface is golden brown. Remove from the oven, leave the tray for a minute for the wafers to firm, then using a spatula, transfer to a wire rack. Bake the remaining wafers in the same way and, when done and cool, pack them in an airtight container.

Garlic dumplings

150g strong white flour (100%)

½ tsp fine sea salt (2%)

100g water at 20°C (67%)

¾ tsp fresh yeast, crumbled (2%)

1 clove garlic, crushed to a paste (3%)

In a bowl, combine the flour and salt, tossing them together with your fingers. In another bowl, whisk together the water and yeast. Stir this liquid in with the flour until you have a soft, sticky dough. Wipe the crushed garlic over the surface of the dough, and work this in roughly. Scrape any dough from your fingers, cover the bowl and leave for 10 minutes.

Rub 1 tsp of corn or olive oil on the work-surface and knead the dough on the oiled surface for 10 seconds, ending with a smooth, round ball. Clean and dry the bowl, then rub lightly with a tsp of oil. Return the dough to the bowl and leave for a further 10 minutes. Remove the dough, knead once more on the oiled surface, returning the shape of the dough to a smooth, round ball. Place it back in the bowl, cover, and leave for 1 hour in a warm (21–25°C) place.

Divide the dough into 12 or so pieces. The weight is not that important, but try to keep them all the same size so that they cook evenly. Lightly oil your hands and roll each piece into a smooth, tight ball. Place these on an oiled tray and cover with a cloth.

Set up your steamer (I use a stack of bamboo ones) or get your braise or broth simmering. Place the dumplings on an oiled plate in the steamer, or drop them into the braise or broth, and cook for 5 minutes, or until the dumplings have puffed up and slightly firmed. To check if they're done, take one out and cut it through with a sharp knife: it should have an open texture and a firm, very moist crumb. Serve immediately, or remove and cool, then heat to boiling when you're ready to serve.

A dumpling is a soft bread, either cooked with or alongside the meal, for example dropped into a thick simmering braise or stew. I have cooked these separately in a small steamer. This way they keep their shape, and look more dignified when plonked on the plate. Good winter fare.

TIP You can substitute half buttermilk (or milk) and half water for the water in the dough to make a richer dumpling.

The fat of
the land

The flavour of a good fat gets even better when it is mixed with the taste of a grain. Equally, a starchy food is improved by the addition of some fat. A flour-thickened sauce gains a richness from butter, just as bacon fat lifts the peppery taste of lentils. But fat can taste excessive without starch, and perhaps it is not the loaf that likes the olive oil, but the oil that likes the loaf. I can eat and enjoy the grain on its own, but the fat often needs something to make it a pleasure.

Starches seem to round out the flavours of meat and fat, just as butter or oil can add a hint of good times to a plain loaf. When we describe this fatted taste as "rounded", what does that mean? Complete, balanced, whole, or simply finished, like the food from childhood, gilded to overcome a fear of plainness? As with hot buttered toast, we mean that the dish becomes good food when the fat is added; finally, and only then, is it ready to be eaten.

Oil worked into dough makes the taste comforting, and we feel wealthy; we add oil because we can afford to; because we have enough to share. We value the fat of the land and include it in breads that are eaten for significant events in our community, whether it is breads for the springtime, before Lent or for Easter, for christenings or weddings, for harvest time or Christmas. The modern affluent-puritan may claim the buttered loaf is an unnecessary extravagance, but for anyone who feels that life is lean enough, these breads make a simple life feel less harsh and more enjoyable.

Sweet butter dough

This is a very simple, very useful butter dough that is handy to make when you have a glut of summer fruit and you need to produce lots of baked goods quickly, such as the apple and custard loaf on page 120. You do need to cover the dough snugly while it sits in the refrigerator overnight, as the high fat content makes it remarkably good at picking up the flavours of other foods nearby. Mine once had the strange taste of smoked sausage. When this is unexpected, it's not so good.

2½ tsp fresh yeast, crumbled (4%)

1 medium egg (12%)

2 medium egg yolks (12%)

125g caster sugar (25%)

500g soft white flour (100%)

200g white leaven (40%)
(see pages 25–7)

125g single cream (25%)

1¼ tsp fine sea salt (2%)

175g unsalted butter (35%)

Crumble the yeast and beat with the egg, egg yolks, and 1 tbsp sugar. Mix in all the remaining ingredients except the butter and knead roughly. Cover and leave for 10 minutes.

Slice the butter into thin pieces, then allow it to soften. Spread the pieces on top of the dough and work them roughly into it. Rub 1 tsp corn or olive oil on the work-surface and knead the dough on the oiled surface for 5 minutes, until the butter is combined and the dough is smooth. Knead the dough into a ball, then place it in a large, tightly-covered container that allows it room to prove, and keep it in the refrigerator.

Use the dough the following day, or at least 18 hours later.

Flaky butter buns

Bread dough layered with good, sweet butter is a constant in the baking traditions of northern Europe. Butter can slow down the rising process, and a way to add richness without losing speed is to layer the butter through the dough rather than kneading it in. This means the fat does not coat the grains of flour and so prevent yeast from accessing sugars to ferment, which is what causes the dough to rise. This is a slow dough, made over two days, weakening the flour and resulting in a tender crumb. On the first day, the dough is mixed, kneaded lightly, and kept in the refrigerator overnight. On the second, the dough is rolled with the butter and made into shapes which are left to rise and then baked.

TIP Let the butter buns rise overnight in the refrigerator, then bake them fresh on a Saturday or Sunday morning. You can also freeze them unbaked, although I've only tried keeping them in the freezer for a week.

500g strong white flour (100%)

1½ tsp fine sea salt (2%)

250g milk at 20°C (50%)

2 tsp fresh yeast, crumbled (2%)

175g unsalted butter (35%)

In a bowl, combine the flour and salt. In another bowl or jug, whisk together the milk and yeast. Pour the liquid in with the dry ingredients and mix with your hands until you have a soft, sticky dough. Scrape any remaining dough from your fingers into the bowl, cover with a cloth, and leave for 10 minutes.

Rub 1 tsp of corn or olive oil on the work-surface and knead the dough on the oiled surface for 10 seconds, ending with a smooth, round ball. Clean and dry the bowl, then rub lightly with a tsp of oil. Return the dough to the bowl and leave for 10 minutes. Remove the dough and knead once more on the oiled surface, returning the shape of the dough to a smooth, round ball. Cover the dough and place in the refrigerator overnight.

The following day, remove the dough from the refrigerator, and leave covered at room temperature (20°C) for 1 hour to lose some of its chill. Remove the butter from the refrigerator, and let that soften to something like the consistency of the dough. On a floured work-surface, roll out the dough until it is a 1cm-thick rectangle. Cut the butter into thin slices and lay it out over two-thirds of the dough. Fold the remaining third back over to cover half the butter, then fold the dough over to cover that. All the butter should now be wrapped up inside the dough. Check that the dough is lightly floured on both sides, then roll out carefully until it is 1cm thick again. Fold the dough in by thirds again, then cover it with a cloth and leave in a cool place for 1 hour.

Roll out the dough once more, but this time fold it in by quarters. The way to do this is by folding each end in so that they meet in the centre, then folding these sides on top of each other (this is called a book fold). Cover the dough and leave to rest in a cool place for a further hour.

To shape the buns, roll the dough out to a 1cm-thick rectangle on a floured surface. Cut circles from the dough measuring 10–12cm in diameter, and pull the edges in towards the centre, pinching them down to get a round or oval bun shape. Place smooth-side-up on a baking tray lined with non-stick baking parchment. Cover with a cloth and leave to rise for 1½ hours in a warm (21–25°C) place.

Preheat the oven to 200°C/400°F/gas mark 6. Bake the butter buns in the centre of the oven for 25 minutes, or until crisp and a light brown in colour. Leave to cool on the tray.

I like to eat these warm, stuffed with a piece of crisp bacon, or you could eat them with honey.

Italy

Italy is a country that I grew up with, from my early teens to my 20s. At the age of 15, I spent a winter in the small Lombardy town of Castellanza, with a family who struggled to get some of the Italian language into my head. Then later, as a photographer in the 1980s, I travelled back and forth, working here and there for a fashion magazine that was based in Milan. My Italian improved, but perhaps not as fast as my affection for the country and its people.

It was Wendy Fogarty, the founder of the British part of the Slow Food movement and an early activist for good bread in Britain, who nudged me to spend some more time in Turin. She'd guide me, prodding me to think about the provenance of the ingredients we bake with, and reminding me of the duty that we bakers have to promote considerate and sustainable agriculture.

To strengthen her argument, Wendy would sit me with young Italians who'd become politicized by the damage they saw in their countryside. Their arguments were both heartfelt and alarming. For me, Wendy, Turin and the Slow Food movement set an example for the way that life could be. Since then, I have become deeply fond of the city, and it is where I now feel most at home in the world.

A few years later, in 2000, with the help of Giovanni Gai from the *Associazione Panificatori Artigiani* (the organization for artisan bakers in Turin) and of the Flour Advisory Bureau in London, I took a group of British bakers to run a small local bakery for the duration of the Slow Food *Salone del Gusto*. We used British flour as well as flour from the artisanal Mulino Marino in Cossano Belbo. We wanted both to learn and to bake together, with no competitive edge and no intention of Union

THIS PAGE, TOP TO BOTTOM: *rubatà chierese*, a *grissini*, at Marta Bera's shop; left to right, their assistant with Marta, Bruna, and their sister; doors in a Turin street; a plaited loaf and a *pane nero* made with rye flour and farro from Marta's shop in Turin's Via San Tommaso. OPPOSITE, CLOCKWISE FROM TOP LEFT: *pane carasau* from Antonio Mura in Buddusò, Sardinia; the dining room at Antiche Sera; Anna Maria of Antiche Sera with her son, Danielle; the interior of Latteria Bera Bruna; *pane di colomba*, a sweet Easter bread; *stirrato Torinese*; *pane di mais*; *pane di olio*; bread at Marta's shop; disks of rosemary and rock salt flatbread called *croccante romana*. CENTRE, CLOCKWISE FROM LEFT: Bruna and a bottle of whey; fresh cheese at Turin's central market; pastry chef Toni Vitiello.

LEFT TO RIGHT: wedges of freshly baked *farinata*; the baker Stella with a tray of *farinata* at Focacceria Tipica Ligure, Turin; chickpea flour batter being poured into a hot baking dish.

Jack waving. It was a period of intense learning and hard work, and marked all of us in one way or another. But subsequently I have returned to Turin often, aided by my pastry chef friend Toni Vitiello, who has been my sturdy guide to excellent breads and baking in the city.

Italian bread is typified by the characteristics of the regional flour, though the "*doppio zero*" rating on each bag is not quite as definitive and helpful as it sounds. When I was working at a small artisan bakery in Milan, I noticed that the baker used two "00" flours. When I asked why, he said, "Well, one is a strong '00' and the other a soft '00' flour." That threw me, as I had always believed that it was enough to simply get Italian "00" flour. It seems that flours vary widely in Italy and bakers there, as in any country, might use two or more flours blended in order to achieve a particular result. At Mulino Marino the flour was stoneground, organic and beige-coloured, and produced beautiful bread with a sweet crust.

The success of a bakery is not simply due to the baker or their bread. The unsung heroes and heroines for every artisan baker are the men and women who sell the bread – those people who turn the experience of buying bread into something softly, or sometimes strictly, pleasurable. Toni Vitiello had insisted that I see the best bread and cheese shops in Turin. Here, three women have the market for bread and cheese stitched up: the Bera sisters. On Via San Tommaso are two shops, on either side of the road, run by the sisters. Two sisters run the Latteria Bera Bruna, which stocks an intensely regional selection of local cheeses, and the third sister, Marta, runs the Panetteria Bera, where most of the fine loaves, *grissini* and crispbreads from Piedmont and elsewhere in Italy can be found. It was Bruna, the oldest sister, who first welcomed me at the Latteria years ago, when I was sourcing whey that I could use while I baked there.

At Marta's Panetteria, the stars are the *grissini* and crispbreads. There are the *grissino stirato del Torinese*, pale golden in colour because of the malt, olive oil and *lardo*, or pork fat, made with soft bread dough that is cut thin and stretched to elongate the aeration. And there are the tightly hand-rolled *rubatà chierese*, pale and almost white, made from a tender biscuit dough that crunches to a powdery crumb.

In every restaurant or *osteria* (the Italian name for a tavern), sticks of either or both *grissini* will sit in the centre of the table. At the Osteria Antiche Sera, one of the best places to taste artisan Piedmont ingredients, Anna Maria and her son Danielle serve the most exquisitely blunt and honest food I have ever eaten, and bread is very much part of the set table. Little bags of crisp *grissini rubatà* sit in the centre of every table, alongside a basket of simple white bread. These are the breads that are eaten with the paper-thin *lardo*, herb-cured lard served on its own, or the soft mountain goat's cheese topped with *salsa verde*.

The Ligurian *farinata* is still sold at a few places in the city. I visit one small bakery where round metal platters are heated and filled with a batter made from chickpea flour, water, salt, and olive oil. After barely 10 minutes in the hot oven the *farinata* emerge, crisp on the surface but almost custard-soft underneath.

There was a time when simple flatbreads such as *farinata* and the Tuscan *castagnaccio*, made from chestnuts, were sold by immigrant street vendors in Turin. Metal pans filled with hot coals were topped with a griddle on which the bread would be cooked. These vendors were typical in Turin through the early 1900s, until the pizza started to gain popularity in the north of Italy. Today, there are very few vendors of these early flatbreads left, and the pizza from Napoli is everywhere. Tastes change, and in the space of a generation some popular traditions can almost be lost.

Olive oil flatbread

330g water at 20°C (66%)	80g extra virgin olive oil (16%)
200g white leaven (40%)	1¼ tsp fresh yeast, crumbled (1%)
(see pages 25–27)	500g strong white flour (100%)
1 tsp ground malt powder (1%)	1½ tsp fine sea salt (2%)

There are bakeries in Genoa that produce this sort of flatbread, known as focaccia. The name is now synonymous with the bubbly, open-textured bread that has become a regular feature in artisan bakeries from San Francisco to London, but seldom is this texture seen in Italy. Usually, the bread is simply made with the house white dough, and it is the shape that defines it. Contemporary artisan bakers work the dough over many hours, so that holes created by the fermenting yeast are stretched and enlarged, giving an exaggerated honeycomb effect. I was always convinced that the texture relied on high-speed mixing, the sort only really possible in commercial bakeries. But, as the bread in the picture shows, it can be made by hand, and simply folded every hour to give this effect. What enhances it, if anything, is a hot oven.

In a bowl or jug, whisk the water with the leaven, malt powder, 30g of the olive oil, and yeast until the mixture is smooth. In another bowl, combine the flour with the salt. Pour the liquid into the dry ingredients and mix them with your hands until you have a soft, sticky dough. Scrape any remaining dough from your fingers into the bowl, cover with a cloth, and leave for 10 minutes.

Tip the remaining olive oil on to a lipped tray and rub it so that the tray is coated. Knead the dough on the tray lightly for 10 seconds, then flip it over so you get a round ball. Cover the dough and leave for a further 10 minutes. Knead the dough on the oiled tray once more, returning the shape of the dough to a smooth, round ball. Place it back in the bowl, cover, and leave for 1 hour in a warm (21–25°C) place.

Rub 1 tsp corn or olive oil on to the work-surface. Pat the dough out into a rectangle on the oiled surface, and fold it in by thirds each way. Flip the dough over so that the seam faces downwards. Cover, and then repeat this patting out and folding every 40 minutes for the next 2 hours. Each time you are gently stretching and folding the dough rather than punching it to knock out the gas. It is important to check that the temperature of the dough does not rise above 21–25°C; it should always feel cool to the touch. When the dough is ready, a cut into the centre should reveal a dramatic network of holes.

Lightly oil two 30 x 20cm baking trays. Cut the dough into two equal pieces, and place each seam-side-down in the centre of a tray, then dimple the surface with your fingertips to slightly flatten it. Don't worry that the dough is only sitting in the centre. Cover the dough and leave for 15 minutes, ideally in a warmer place near the oven at 25–28°C.

Preheat the oven to 220°C/425°F/gas mark 7. Uncover the dough and stretch it out so that it covers more of the tray. To do this, lift the dough at each side and pull it out towards the edge of the tray as far as it will go. I usually cover the dough again at this point and leave it for a further 10 minutes before stretching it one last time to fully cover the tray. Drizzle a little olive oil and sprinkle coarse sea salt over the surface, then make deep impressions with your fingertips pressing down into the dough right to the tray.

Bake the bread in the centre of the oven for 35 minutes, or until the upper surface is a good golden brown. Using a spatula, ease the bread from the tray and let it cool on a wire rack.

Soft curd loaf

Fresh cheese, made from the curd strained from full-fat milk (see page 45) can be crumbled into the mixing liquid and used to enrich and fatten the crumb of the loaf. This loaf can make use of other crumbly cheeses such as Cheshire or Wensleydale. If it is summer and you have too many chives, finely chop a handful and add these to the dough.

300g water at 20°C (60%)

2 tsp fresh yeast, crumbled (2%)

125g soft curd cheese, eg ricotta (25%)

250g plain flour (50%)

250g strong white flour (50%)

1½ tsp fine sea salt (2%)

In a bowl or jug, whisk together the water, yeast, and curd cheese. In a large bowl, combine the two flours with the salt. Pour the liquid into the dry ingredients and stir until you have a soft, sticky dough.

Rub 1 tsp of corn or olive oil on to the work-surface and knead the dough on the oiled surface for 10 seconds, ending with a smooth, round ball. Clean and dry the bowl, then rub lightly with a tsp of oil. Return the dough to the bowl and leave for a further 10 minutes. Remove the dough and knead once more on the oiled surface, returning the shape of the dough to a smooth, round ball. Place it back in the bowl, cover, and leave for 1 hour in a warm (21–25°C) place.

Grease and flour a deep 12x19cm loaf tin. Shape the loaf into a baton (see page 21). Lower it neatly into the prepared tin, then cover with a cloth and leave to rise for 1½ hours, or until almost doubled in height.

Preheat the oven to 210°C/410°F/gas mark 6½. Dust the top of the loaf with flour and bake for 15 minutes, then lower the heat to 180°C/350°F/gas mark 4 and bake for a further 25–30 minutes, or until the top of the loaf is a shiny dark brown and the loaf has come away from the sides of the tin. Remove from the tin and cool on a wire rack.

Chickpea pancakes

My friend Toni Vitiello, a very good pastry chef from Turin, took me to his favourite bakery one afternoon to eat *farinata* with him. *Farinata* is a traditional Ligurian pancake made with chickpea flour and olive oil, from the same school as the English Yorkshire pudding and almost identical to the Provençal *socca*. So this baker removed great trays covered in the blistered yellow flatbread (the sulphurous colour comes from both the chickpea flour and the olive oil) from the oven and cut wedges for us before wrapping them in sheets of paper. I would be lying if I said I loved my first mouthful; I spat it into the bin. "What? This was the food I grew up on!" said Toni. So I ate another piece and another. Now every time I go back, I buy more *farinata* and I'm half-way through my training and getting close to loving it.

200g chickpea flour (100%)

200g water at 20°C (100%)

½ tsp fine sea salt (1%)

50g olive oil (25%)

2 tbsp olive oil for frying

a small sprig of rosemary, chopped

In a bowl, beat together the flour, water, and salt until you have a smooth batter. Cover and leave for 2 hours.

Preheat the oven to 220°C/425°F/gas mark 7. Add the olive oil to the batter and beat well until combined. Take a large, flat pan, such as a *paella* pan, and add the 2 tbsp of olive oil. Heat this on top of the stove until the oil is smoking, then sprinkle in the rosemary. Let this sizzle for a moment, then pour in the batter. Remove the pan from the heat, place it in the hot oven, then shut the door and leave for 20 minutes. By this time the pancake should be slightly puffed and lightly brown on top.

Remove the *farinata* from the oven, let it cool in the tray for a moment, then put it on a chopping board and cut into squares or wedges to spread with something like tapenade, or serve with a bowl of good olives and a Negroni.

Sage, cheese, and shallot pie

Sometimes bread can encase the meal. In this recipe, whole shallots are baked in the oven and then left to cool before being halved and mixed with melted butter, chopped sage, and cheese. This mixture is baked between two discs of bread dough to make a substantial supper dish. I like adding cubes of cooked beetroot when it is in season, as their earthy taste adds vigour to the loaf. The olive oil dough used in this recipe is the same as for the flatbread on page 151. Simply halve all the quantities to produce around 550g of dough, and follow the mixing and kneading instructions in the first two paragraphs of that recipe, so that you have a smooth ball of dough which has rested for 1 hour.

FOR THE FILLING:

12 medium shallots, unpeeled (43%)

50g unsalted butter (9%)

a dozen sage leaves (0.5%)

250g good goat's cheese (45%)

fine sea salt and ground black pepper

FOR THE DOUGH:

550g olive oil dough (100%) (see page 151 and recipe introduction note)

Preheat the oven to 180°C/350°F/gas mark 4. Place the shallots on a baking sheet and roast for 40 minutes, or until a knife pierces the flesh easily. To conserve fuel, I like to do this when the oven is on for another purpose, such as cooking the supper. Leave the shallots in the refrigerator overnight for use the following day.

Carefully peel the tough brown outer layers of skin from the cold shallots, leaving the tender, purple-ish bulbs. Cut these in half. Melt the butter and mix with the shallots, the sage (torn into pieces), and the goat's cheese (chopped into rough cubes). Place this to one side while you roll out the dough.

Rub 1 tsp of olive oil on to the work-surface. Divide the dough into two equal pieces and, on the oiled surface, roll each into a 40 x 20cm oval. Place one of these on a suitably sized oiled baking sheet. Spread the shallot mixture evenly over the base, season with salt and pepper, then lay the other piece of dough on top. Seal it well at the edges, then press the top sheet of dough down at several points across its surface to seal it to the base. Using a sharp knife, cut five or six air vents in the top of the dough for steam to escape. Lightly cover the pie with a cloth and leave for 40 minutes.

Preheat the oven to 220°C/425°F/gas mark 7. Bake in the centre of the oven for 40 minutes, or until the bread is crisp and golden. Either serve hot or leave until warm – but this pie is best eaten before it gets cold.

Brown butter picklets

100g wholewheat flour (50%)	¾ tsp fresh yeast, crumbled (2%)
100g plain white flour (50%)	50g butter (25%)
½ tsp fine sea salt (1%)	1 tsp bicarbonate of soda (2.5%)
100g milk at 20°C (50%)	1 tbsp extra water (8%)
100g water at 20°C (50%)	oil, lard, or butter for frying

In a bowl, combine the white and wholewheat flours with the salt. In another bowl, mix the milk and water with the yeast. Pour the liquid into the dry ingredients, then beat well until smooth. Cover the bowl and leave for 2 hours, until the mixture is bubbly.

Place the butter in a saucepan and heat until it is nut-brown, then remove the pan from the heat and pour the butter into a small bowl to cool slightly and stop cooking. (You could simply run cold water across the underside of the pan to lower the heat quickly.) Beat the browned butter into the yeasted batter until it is evenly combined. Mix the soda with the 1 tbsp of water and stir into the batter.

Preheat a non-stick frying pan, and in it heat 1 tsp of oil, lard or butter until it is almost smoking hot. Rub this evenly around the surface with a ball of paper towel. Lower the heat and put 1–2 tbsp of batter into the pan per picklet, cooking two or three in the pan at a time. Cook until the edges are crisp and brown and the surface is broken with air bubbles that break through to the base of the pan – a minute or so. Using a spatula, loosen each picklet from the frying pan and flip over. Cook each picklet for another minute, or until both sides are brown. Remove from the pan, place on a plate, and cover with a cloth while you cook the remaining picklets.

My mother had a large aluminium electric frying pan called a Sunbeam, which used to be brought out every Saturday to make pikelets, what I knew to be tiny pancakes made with milk, egg, and butter. But there is an earlier version, almost forgotten now, with the slightly different spelling of "picklet", which was a version of the crumpet. This was a leavened bread cooked on a griddle and served warm with a little butter or jam.

Garlic and goose fat pancakes

These little pancakes, made with cooked potato, goose fat, and garlic, can be stacked on a plate and served with crisp herring roes and a glass of something good. They are best made and eaten quickly, though they can be wrapped in foil and placed in a hot oven to reheat.

150g millet flour (50%)

150g plain white flour (50%)

¾ tsp fine sea salt (2%)

100g cooked potato, sieved (33%)

125g water at 20°C (42%)

1 tsp fresh yeast, crumbled (2%)

30g goose fat or lard (10%)

1 clove garlic, cut into slivers

2 tbsp chopped parsley

In a large bowl, combine the two flours with the salt. In another bowl or jug, whisk the sieved potato with the water and yeast. Pour the liquid into the dry ingredients, mixing well until you have a smooth, thick batter. Leave at room temperature for 2 hours, or until frothy.

In a saucepan, heat the goose fat and garlic over a low heat for 2–3 minutes so that the garlic barely colours. Pour this into the batter, stirring well so that the oil does not get a chance to cook the mixture. Stir in the parsley.

Preheat a non-stick frying pan, and in it heat 1 tsp of oil, lard or butter until it is almost smoking hot. Rub this evenly around the surface with a ball of paper towel. Lower the heat and put 1 tbsp of batter into the pan per pancake, cooking three or four in the pan at a time. Cook until the edges are crisp and brown and the surface is broken with air bubbles that break through to the base of the pan – about a minute. Using a spatula, loosen each pancake from the frying pan and flip over. Cook each pancake for another minute, or until both sides are brown. Remove from the pan, place on a plate, and cover with a cloth while you cook the remaining pancakes.

Lard cake

There are many versions of this famous bread made with lard or clarified dripping. Some contain currants or sultanas, but the version here is simpler. Susan Beaty-Pownall, who edited a series of cookbooks for *Queen* magazine in the early 20th-century, gives a recipe for lard cake which simply uses lard and sugar. To my taste, this plain cake is more adaptable and I would serve it with something like figs or rum-soaked currants.

TIP Buy your lard from a good butcher and try to insist that it is unadulterated pork lard, which has a much better flavour than the cheap blocks.

500g strong white flour (100%)	2½ tsp fresh yeast, crumbled (2%)
1½ tsp fine sea salt (2%)	150g pork lard (30%)
200g white leaven (40%)	150g caster sugar (30%)
(see pages 25–27)	scraping of nutmeg
250g water at 20°C (50%)	2 tbsp caster sugar for dredging

In a large bowl, combine the flour and the salt. In another bowl or jug, whisk together the leaven, water, and yeast. Pour the liquid into the dry ingredients and stir until you have a soft, sticky dough. Scrape any remaining dough from your fingers into the bowl, cover and leave for 10 minutes.

Rub 1 tsp of corn or olive oil on to the work-surface and knead the dough on the oiled surface for 10 seconds, ending with a smooth, round ball. Clean and dry the bowl, then rub with a tsp of oil. Return the dough to the bowl, cover, and leave for a further 10 minutes. Remove the dough, knead once more on the oiled surface, returning the shape of the dough to a smooth, round ball. Place it back in the bowl, cover, and leave for 1 hour in a warm (21–25°C) place.

On a floured work-surface, roll the dough out until it is a 1cm-thick rectangle. Cut the lard into thin slices and lay it out over two-thirds of the dough. Sprinkle the sugar evenly over the lard, then fold the remaining third of the dough back over to cover half the lard, then fold the dough over to cover that. All of the lard and sugar should now be wrapped up inside the dough. Check that the dough is lightly floured on both sides, then roll the dough out carefully until it is again a 1cm-thick rectangle. Fold the dough in by thirds once more, then cover it with a cloth and leave in a cool place for 30 minutes.

Roll the dough out on the work-surface until it is again about a 1cm-thick rectangle. Roll the dough up from one end into a tight cylinder, then leave it to sit on the work-surface, covered, for 10 minutes.

Line a 25cm spring-form cake tin (or a similar ovenproof tin) with non-stick baking parchment. Using a sharp knife, cut through the cylinder of dough lengthways. Then, with the cut surface facing upward, spiral the dough around. Working carefully, as this is a bit tricky, lift this spiral and plonk it down inside the tin, cut-side-upwards. Cover the tin and leave the dough in a warm (25°C) place for 1 hour, or until almost doubled in height.

Preheat the oven to 200°C/400°F/gas mark 6. Sprinkle the nutmeg over the surface, then dredge the upper surface with 2 tbsp of caster sugar. Bake in the centre of the oven for 20 minutes, then reduce the heat to 180°C/350°F/gas mark 4 and bake for a further 40 minutes, or until the top is a good dark brown, verging on burnt. Leave the cake to cool in the tin for 15 minutes before carefully transferring it to a wire rack to cool. Wrap in greaseproof paper to store.

England

A food writer once complained bitterly to me about bread in England. It was an opinion coloured by one visit, one city, and one baker, as if a stop-over tourist had judged British food by the restaurants at Heathrow. There is good bread in England, but it isn't celebrated and we're not self-congratulatory by habit. You just need to know where to look.

In London there's Troels Bendix at Breadsetcetera in Wandsworth, Gail Stephen's standard setting Baker & Spice in Knightsbridge and Queen's Park, Sally Clarke's eponymous bakery in Notting Hill, partners Rachel Duffield and Liz Weisberg at the Lighthouse bakery near Clapham Junction, Matt Jones at Flourpower in Dulwich, and Manuel Monade and his wood-fired Llopis oven at Born & Bread in Peckham. Outside London, there's the Café Royal Bakery in Newcastle, Hobbs House Bakery in Chipping Sodbury, and Peter Cook at S. C. Price and Sons in Ludlow. And there are many more making good bread quietly, without fanfare or even much local praise.

Bridport, a beautiful town near the west Dorset coast, is the home of Leakers. Aidan Chapman's bakery is situated behind a narrow high-street shop front, with windows along one side so that the bakery is lit by the morning sun rising. Running back along the right-hand wall is an old deck oven, once oil-fired but now run with electricity. Every morning this oven produces leaven breads, crusty top-split tin loaves to make a fine English sandwich, semolina-crusted cobs, "winter warmers" made with local ale and hard cheese, egg-glazed Bath buns, and yeast pastries layered with local farm butter. It's early morning and a queue has formed already, mostly of customers who know exactly what they want and how it should be baked.

THIS PAGE FROM TOP RIGHT: an old mill stone at Cann Mill, Dorset; Jack Lang holds a 100 per cent leaven bread, fresh from his wood-fired home oven. LEFT: baker Emmanuel Hadjiandreou holds a barrel of leaven flutes at Daylesford Farm Shop, Gloucestershire. OPPOSITE PAGE, CLOCKWISE FROM TOP LEFT: 32kg sacks of stone-milled flour at Cann Mill; two rye breads rise in linen-lined baskets on Lang's kitchen table; miller Michael Stoate; Lang's loaves cooling next to a bowl of English butter; the knobbly top of a grain loaf coming out of Lang's oven; pizza-making in the garden; Cann Mills' office sign. CENTRE: a thick layer of fragrant thyme growing on the warm roof of Lang's oven.

CANN MILLS

OPEN MONDAY - FRIDAY
8.30am - 5.00pm
CLOSED 1.00pm - 2.00pm
AND ALL DAY TUESDAY

PLEASE RING AND / OR PRESS BELL →

"A growing number of bakers... [are] keen to develop baking methods to suit locally grown grain."

I ask Aidan about the provenance of his ingredients. "We have a farmer around the corner who supplies our vegetables, pears, and the soft loganberries for these tarts," he says. "We use a local cider for our apple rye bread, and the same ciderman supplies the apples for our tarts. Customers also bring in fruit from their garden, and we give them some of whatever we make from it in return."

Like a growing number of bakers in Britain, Aidan sees the flour he uses as intrinsic to the flavour and character of the loaf and is keen to develop baking methods to suit locally grown grain and turn the resulting flour into a perfect loaf. Such loaves have a different crumb and crust to ones made with imported flour, and a beauty all of their own.

The greatest impact on artisan baking in England over the last 20 years has come from millers such as John Lister at Shipton Mill, Michael and Clare Marriage at Doves Farm, and first Norman Stoate and now his son Michael at Cann Mills. They have given practical support to organic farmers by buying and milling their grain, and have made available flour from locally grown, unusual, and historic varieties of cereal. Their dedicated work has found its champions in a new generation of bakers.

At Daylesford in Gloucestershire, baker Emmanuel Hadjiandreou is working with Michael Stoate, who mills their harvest of Hereward and Maris Widgeon wheat, so that the loaves come from the surrounding land. "We were growing wheat for cow feed," says Emmanuel, "and I said: 'Why don't we try growing wheat for milling?' Though the farmer was very doubtful, we had a sample of Hereward milled and it produced a great loaf – nutty, sweet, heavy, but not doughy." Along with the bakery and farm shop, Daylesford includes a creamery producing award-winning cheeses, a greengrocer, a butcher, and a small dining hall, all using produce from two local estates. This well-funded endeavour is just what you might hope for from a local government initiative but is, instead, supported by the efforts of one family: the Bamfords.

Like the artisan on the high street, many home-bakers like going after excellence and a primitive baking experience: grinding the wheat for freshly milled flour, nursing a natural starter through its infancy to full-blown fermentation, and blending grains and flours to create a personal mix. Jack Lang, "Entrepreneur in Residence" at the University of Cambridge, is a passionate baker down to the wood-fired oven in his garden. "Traditional wood-fired ovens are good at maintaining steady, even heat, and are economical," says Jack. "Equally, naturally leavened breads are easy to manage, especially for the home-baker, as the dough matures more slowly and the point when the loaf gets to the oven is less critical."

LEFT TO RIGHT: baker Aidan Chapman holding his rye and local cider loaf; Aidan and trainee Caroline Rouiller standing outside the bakery in Bridport, Dorset.

White loaf with grated chestnuts

The large amount of fat left over when you roast a duck or goose has traditionally been used to enrich other foods, preserve meats, and even sipped by the warm spoonful to ease congestion. It was used, and not wasted. In this recipe, shallots are softened in duck fat, then stirred into the dough with grated chestnuts.

TIP You can substitute vacuum-packed cooked whole chestnuts, available all year round, for the freshly toasted chestnuts in the recipe.

75g duck fat (15%)

2 small shallots, finely chopped (6%)

200g fresh chestnuts, roasted, peeled and finely grated (40%)

500g strong white flour (100%)

1½ tsp fine sea salt (2%)

300g water at 20°C (60%)

1¼ tsp fresh yeast, crumbled (1%)

200g rye leaven (40%) (see pages 25–27 and 31)

Melt the duck fat in a saucepan, then cook the finely chopped shallots in the fat until they begin to sizzle. Lower the heat, cover with a lid, and cook for 5 minutes, or until the shallots have softened and become almost translucent. Remove from the heat, stir in the chestnuts and leave to cool until warm.

In a bowl, combine the flour with the salt. In another bowl or jug, mix the water with the yeast and rye leaven. Add the liquid to the dry ingredients and stir with your hands until you have a soft, sticky dough. Scrape any remaining dough from your fingers into the bowl, cover and leave for 10 minutes. Add the chestnut and shallot mixture, squidging it well into the dough with your fingers to mix it as evenly as possible. Cover the dough again and leave for a further 10 minutes.

Rub 1 tsp of corn or olive oil on the work-surface and knead the dough on the oiled surface for 10 seconds, ending with a smooth, round ball. Clean and dry the bowl, then rub lightly with a tsp of oil. Return the dough to the bowl and leave for a further 10 minutes. Remove the dough and knead once more on the oiled surface, returning the dough to the shape of a smooth, round ball. Place it back in the bowl, cover, and leave for 1 hour in a warm (21–25°C) place.

Dust two tea-towels with rye flour, and line two 20 x 10cm oblong loaf tins with these. They will act as the proving baskets (or use flour-dusted wicker baskets, if you have them). Divide the dough into two equal pieces. Shape each piece into a baton (see page 21) and sit it seam-side-up inside the cloth. Cover the upper surface with another cloth and leave to prove for 2 hours.

Preheat the oven to 220°C/425°F/gas mark 7. Carefully up-turn the loaves on to a flour-dusted baking sheet and, using a sharp blade, slash the dough diagonally two or three times. Bake in the centre of the oven for 45 minutes, until each loaf is a good rich brown colour and sounds hollow when tapped on the bottom. Remove from the oven and leave to cool on a wire rack.

Fried flatbread with dill seeds and pork crackling

250g strong white flour (100%)

¾ tsp fine sea salt (2%)

1 tsp dill seeds (2%)

150g water at 20°C (60%)

2 tsp fresh yeast, crumbled (2%)

100g soft pork crackling or rendered

beef scraps, finely chopped (40%)

lard or dripping for brushing and frying

A good rib of beef will usually have some bits of slightly gristly fat, which don't completely render down, even after roasting. Likewise, the crackling on some cuts of pork will remain soft and chewy, rather than become the crisp, tasty accompaniment to a roast dinner. We might discard these scraps, but in Russia and the Ukraine I've seen home-cooks save them to use in a beetroot soup or when baking. This recipe is based on a traditional bread made for me by Farkhat and Saodat, a young Uzbek couple working in Moscow. They used beef fat, which gave the loaf a rich, meaty taste. As the dough is mixed cold, the rendered scraps won't release any extra fat until the bread is cooked. It makes an excellent thin bread, perfect with a boiled gammon joint or a roast.

TIP You can make these rendered scraps at home by cutting the excess fat from a joint of pork or beef into small cubes and roasting them in the oven. This will also give you a bowl of dripping.

In a large bowl, roughly combine the flour, salt, and dill seeds. In another bowl or jug, whisk the water with the yeast. Stir the liquid into the dry ingredients and mix with your hands until you have a soft, sticky dough. Mix the chopped crackling into the dough. Scrape any remaining dough from your fingers into the bowl, cover and leave for 10 minutes.

Rub 1 tsp of corn or olive oil on to the work-surface and knead the dough on the oiled surface for 10 seconds, ending with a smooth, round ball. Clean and dry the bowl, then rub lightly with a tsp of oil. Return the dough to the bowl and leave for a further 10 minutes. Remove the dough and knead once more on the oiled surface, ending up with the dough in the shape of a smooth, round ball. Place it back in the bowl, cover, and leave for 1 hour in a warm (21–25°C) place.

Lightly flour the work-surface and roll the dough out into a 40 x 20cm rectangle. Lightly brush the surface of the dough with melted lard, then cut the dough lengthways into four strips, each measuring 40 x 5cm. Roll one strip up tightly, then continue to roll the next strip where the last ended, continuing this rolling until all the strips have been used. Sit the coil of dough on its end and, using the ball of your hand, bash the coil flat. Check that it's not sticking, and dust underneath and over the dough with additional flour, then roll the dough out again, this time into a circle to cover the base of the frying pan. Cover the dough on the work-surface and leave it to rise for 30 minutes.

Place 1 tbsp of lard in a wide, heavy-based frying pan and leave it over a gentle heat to get hot. Carefully lower the disc of dough into the pan and fry it gently over a low heat. I use a heat diffuser ring over a low flame and move the pan on to this once the dough is in it – this stops the heat burning a spot in the centre of the bread. With a pair of tongs, lift the edge of the dough after 2 minutes to make sure it is colouring well but not burning. If it is browning too quickly, reduce the heat. After 4 minutes, flip the dough over and cook the other side for the same length of time. Once cooked, transfer the bread to a warm plate and serve.

The dry breads of winter

Grain and flour are hard to store for long periods without damp and vermin turning them into something less palatable. Moist grains sprout during the wet winter months, flour moulds or mildews, and soft breads stale and harden. But if the flour is made into breads rolled thin and baked crisp, the grain has been converted into food that stores well and is always ready to be eaten. As a primitive convenience food, the dry biscuit, cracker and crispbread once helped nourish communities through the long winter months until the spring, when the soil would again provide green food.

Today we make these breads because of their taste, their convenience and the way in which they can combine with other foods. Often they are leavened with soda or yeast, creating a softer crunch. Though we now tend to judge flour by how well it can produce light, aerated bread, these traditional flatbreads only really work with the less glutinous flours that cannot produce elastic and resilient dough; if the flour is too strong, the result is leathery. Flours such as rye, barley, oat, and buckwheat make generously flavoured crispbreads with a tender texture.

These breads are less demanding on our home ovens as they need a drier heat and don't need the explosive temperatures and steamy atmosphere that suit crusty, open-textured breads. Some, such as the oatcakes, are fully dried in the oven. Others, such as the dark crisp rye bread, might need crisping up before eating (just pop them in the toaster or a hot oven for a few minutes). All of them can be made simply by hand and require little more baking equipment than a flat metal baking tray.

Dark crisp rye bread

Slightly salty, hard, and brittle, rye breads such as these were once the mainstay of life in Sweden. During World War II, these breads, called *knäckebröd*, were a dry ration supplied to soldiers. Sweden's most contemporary bakers still produce different versions. Starkly modern in appearance, such breads are very popular. One of the best artisan producers of *knäckebröd* is Robert Saberski's Roslagsbröd bakery in Gimo, north of Stockholm. Baker Leif Torstensson studiously watches over the yellow-painted machines chugging away as they stretch and roll the wet sticky dough into dimpled sheets, finally appearing as round discs with a hole in the middle. Traditionally, a pole was threaded through the hole to hang the breads by the fire to dry and crisp.

TIP I've used a little rye leaven in the mix, which gently sours the dough and emphasises the natural tang of the rye flour. But it is more common to only use commercial yeast so, if you like, leave the leaven out. Try altering the coarseness of the rye flour that you use. Stoneground rye, though difficult to work into a leavened rye bread, works well as a crisp rye bread.

200g water at 20°C (100%)

½ tsp fresh yeast, crumbled (1%)

100g rye leaven (50%)
(see pages 25–27 and 31)

200g fine or wholemeal rye flour (100%)

¾ tsp fine sea salt (2%)

In a bowl, whisk together the water, yeast, and leaven. In another bowl, combine the flour and salt. Stir the dry ingredients into the yeasted mixture until you have a thick paste. Cover and leave for 3 hours, until the mixture has risen.

Tear a piece of baking parchment into two pieces, each large enough to cover a 30 x 20cm baking tray. Place one sheet of paper on the work-surface and scrape half of the batter on to it. Dredge the batter-dough heavily with rye flour and roll it out to 5–8mm thick, dusting the top of the dough with more rye flour should it even hint at sticking to the rolling pin. Transfer the dough-covered paper on to a baking tray, then repeat with the other half of the mixture. Cover both trays with a dry cloth and leave in a warm (23–28°C) place for about 2 hours, or until doubled in height.

Preheat the oven to 220°C/425°F/gas mark 7. With the end of a pencil or a wooden spoon, stab at the surface of the rye dough to make dimples all over it. Repeat with the other sheet, then use a sharp knife to cut 10cm squares in the dough. Bake each tray for 40–50 minutes, or until the upper surface is lightly tipped with golden patches against the grey rye crust.

Leave to cool on a wire rack overnight so that the rye breads become dry and brittle. Break into squares and pack into an airtight container.

Light rye flatbread

These round flatbreads, made with a combination of rye and white wheat flours, can be baked quickly and kept soft if covered with a cloth. This is how they would traditionally be made in Finland. Otherwise they can be made brittle, and more suited to dunking into a broth or a braise, by leaving them in the oven for 15 minutes longer.

TIP After baking for 20 minutes, the flatbreads can be removed from the oven and quickly split with a serrated knife, then returned to the hot oven to crisp. This turns the breads into thin rusks, good to serve with cured fish, marinated vegetables or soft cheeses.

300g strong white flour (75%)

100g fine rye flour (25%)

1 tsp fine sea salt (2%)

300g water at 20°C (75%)

1½ tsp fresh yeast, crumbled (1.5%)

3 tsp honey (3%)

In a bowl, combine the two flours with the salt. In another bowl or jug, whisk the water with the yeast and honey. Mix the liquid into the dry ingredients, squeezing the dough through your fingertips until evenly but roughly combined. Cover and leave for 10 minutes.

Rub 1 tsp of corn or olive oil on the work-surface and knead the dough gently on the oiled surface for 10–15 seconds. Return the dough to the bowl, cover and leave for 10 minutes. Remove the dough from the bowl and knead once more on the oiled surface for 10–15 seconds. Place it back in the bowl, cover and leave for 10 minutes, then knead one final time for 10–15 seconds.

Give the dough a turn (see page 19), and repeat after 45 and 90 minutes.

By this time it should be puffy and the surface blistered with bubbles. On a well-floured surface, roll the dough out to a thickness of 8mm. Using a 10cm round cutter (I use a sharp edged plastic bowl), press down into the dough to create discs. Remove each disc and place them, spaced a few centimetres apart, on floured baking trays. Cover with a cloth. Lightly re-knead the trimmings so that the dough is smooth again. Cover and leave for 10 minutes before rolling and cutting into the final discs. Leave the dough discs for 1½ hours, or until almost doubled in height.

Preheat the oven to 200°C/400°F/gas mark 6. With floured fingertips, make dimples in the surface of each dough disc. Bake in the centre of the oven for 25–30 minutes, or until the surface is gently coloured. Slide the discs on to a cooling rack. If you prefer the breads softish, cover them with a cloth while they cool.

Salt crackers

These crisp, flaky, brittle flatbreads are made from a yeasty dough layered with a mixture of butter, flour and bicarbonate of soda. You need a soft flour to make the best biscuits, so be on the look-out for flour milled from local varieties, which are usually soft in Britain, as they will produce a biscuit with a tender bite. Failing that, replace 25g of the flour used in the dough with cornflour or potato starch.

TIP One forgotten biscuit, the Cumberland cream cracker, included caraway seeds in the mixture. This was typical of many savoury biscuits made at the start of the 20th-century, such as Wiggs and the original Dr Abernethy's biscuit. Try seeding the top with either caraway, mustard or dill seeds together with salt.

FOR THE ROLLING CRUMBS:

25g soft white flour (100%)

½ tsp fine sea salt (1%)

½ tsp bicarbonate of soda (1%)

10g unsalted butter or good lard (40%)

FOR THE DOUGH:

½ tsp fresh yeast, crumbled (2%)

125g water at 20°C (62%)

200g soft white flour (100%)

½ tsp fine sea salt (1%)

fine sea salt for dusting the biscuits

FOR THE ROLLING CRUMBS In a bowl, combine the flour with the salt and bicarbonate of soda. Rub the butter into the dry ingredients until the mixture resembles a fine crumble mix. Leave at room temperature while you prepare the other ingredients.

FOR THE DOUGH In a bowl or jug, whisk the yeast with the water. In another bowl, combine the flour with the salt. Stir the dry ingredients into the liquid and combine the mixture into a dough.

Rub 1 tsp of corn or olive oil on the work-surface and knead the dough on the oiled surface for 10–15 seconds. Return it to the bowl, cover and leave for 15 minutes, then knead briefly once more. Place the dough back in the bowl, cover and leave for 2 hours, until it has almost doubled in size.

On a floured work-surface, roll the dough out into a 5mm-thick 30 x 20cm rectangle, with the longest side facing you. Sprinkle the buttered flour rolling crumbs over two-thirds of the dough, then fold the remaining third back into the centre. Fold the dough over once more so the crumbs are encased in the dough. Seal the edges of the dough, then roll it once more to measure 30 x 20cm. Fold the dough in thirds again, then cover with a cloth and leave for 30 minutes.

Roll the dough out until it is 3–4mm thick. Prick the surface of the dough with a fork. Cut squares from the dough, and place them on a baking sheet. I bake these a trayful at a time, rolling and cutting more as the previous ones bake.

Preheat the oven to 200°C/400°F/gas mark 6. Lightly brush the top of the biscuits with water and, using a tea-strainer and 1 tsp of salt, finely dust the top of the dough. Bake in the centre of the oven for 30 minutes, or until the biscuits are crisp, dry, and lightly coloured on top. Transfer to a wire cooling rack, then bake the remaining dough.

Eat with slivers of good cheese or crumble roughly into something like a thick fish soup.

France

Long ago, many grand hotels contained their own bakeries. As with the old cruise ships, all of the cooking was carried out down in the depths, beneath the suites and rooms, by a vast coterie of talented chefs. Bread was rarely purchased already baked by these hotels. Dough would be mixed and baked through the night so that freshly made breads, made to perfected house recipes, were ready for every meal. These hotel kitchens were also training grounds for young apprentices – people who could learn a variety of skills from some of the finest craftsmen in their field. Few hotels operate in this way now; it has become more economical for them to buy in prepared ingredients, and sometimes meals, too. But in a few hotels, chefs continue to bake with a brilliant vigour.

It's night, and the bakers are at work in the basement of the Hôtel Plaza Athénée in Paris. The guests are asleep in their rooms upstairs when I arrive, just as the bakers are starting their shifts. Getting up at night for work is a strange task. The instinct is to stay very quiet, dodging the drunks and late-night party goers in order to weave a path to work. Night-bakers creep about in darkness, quietly turning keys and shutting doors, mumbling at bus drivers or taxi guys, only really awakening in the bright light of the noisy bakery and with the radiated warmth from the oven.

The Plaza Athénée is the Paris home of France's most revered contemporary chef de cuisine, Alain Ducasse. He is a talented, feisty maverick, who insists that the whole meal in his restaurant be extraordinary, and that the best bread be served with it. Since the restaurant is an asset to the hotel, the bakery is too, and is allowed to be excellent without too much hindrance from the money men. Nicolas Berger is the chef pâtissier for Alain Ducasse, and runs the pâtisserie and the bakery as part of his charge. Nicolas's work involves perfecting the recipes and keeping the output of each commis chef consistent, on time, and astounding.

I've come here on a pilgrimage to see a roll. It is a special, beautiful, spiky bread roll, with charred pointed ends and a bulbous middle that has been slashed twice with a blade. This is the most imitated roll that I know of, and replicas are seen in artisan bakeries around the world. The shape shows plainly that such rolls have not popped out of a machine as little dough balls. The tapered points can only be made by hand. They are fragile, baked in a

ABOVE, CLOCKWISE FROM TOP: Bakers working for Alain Ducasse; *petit pain* left to rise on a board; the Hôtel Plaza Athénée's lobby door, opulent with mirrors, gilding, and crystal. OPPOSITE, CLOCKWISE FROM TOP RIGHT: Head baker David Marquès; *petit epi*; the new classic dinner roll; freshly baked baguettes; David cuts the dough into a wheatsheaf shape; David rolling the pointed ends on the dinner roll; the rolls resting on a linen cloth. CENTRE: a waiter places a roll on a restaurant table.

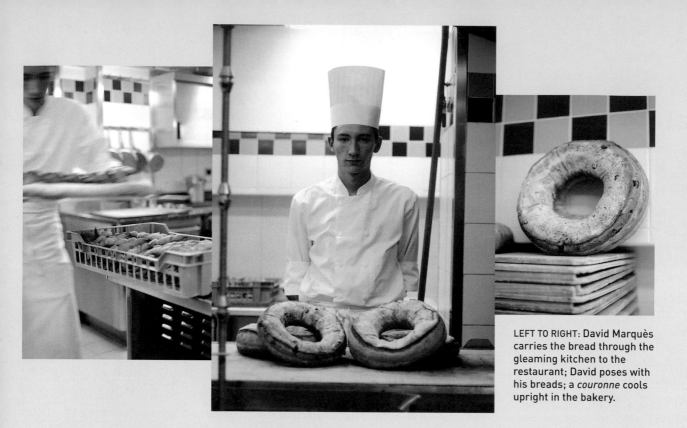

hot oven so that the edges are singed black, and possess a crust that is thin, golden and crisp.

Because of the large number of rolls that the bakery makes, there is a machine to assist the combining of the dough. The flour, salt, water, and leavening are mixed very slowly in a machine called a petrin. The word "petrin" simply means mixer, but this type of mixer is a world away from the high-speed machines that have driven post-war baking. A pair of curved steel prongs gently flip the dough up and over, again and again, and the action of the dough rotates the bowl as it spins freely on a central pivot.

The petrin imitates the hand labour of a baker, gently stretching the dough with each rotation. There is nothing aggressive, energetic or aerobic here; just a quiet knead and a gentle pull. Leaven is added, but it is stored as dough rather than as a batter, and added only after the dough has been mixed and been left to rest. As the action of even this mixer is still more aggressive than that of the gentler hand, this delay in adding the leaven prevents over-stressing.

David Marquès is the young baker in charge of producing these rolls. All the bakers are immaculately groomed, with their crisp, white uniforms tied and tucked in closely. Twenty years ago in London, a young chef called Marco Pierre White worked in a uniform that looked like he'd been the victor of a food fight, and the sweat, grime, and dishevelled appearance said "I am not a repressed robot but a vigorous chef who cares more about flavour than about personal appearance". But for one of him, a thousand others simply saw the grime as a masculine symbol, and today imitate the look rather than the effort and excellence that lay behind it. Here, David and the other bakers work clean and hard.

The dough for the rolls is shaped in stages. First, pieces of dough are weighed and pulled into small balls. This gives the baker an even shape to mould. After a short rest, the dough is rolled against a wooden surface. The heel of each hand stretches and rolls thin points on the ends of the rolls, and they are then left to rest on linen-covered trays. The long, shiny fibres in the linen stop the dough from sticking; cotton can leave woolly fibres in dough. Once the dough has risen slightly, David cuts the rolls with a sharp blade, then puts them straight into the oven at a high temperature. This causes the rolls to puff into buxom fullness, tearing along the cuts and charring on the tapered ends. They finally arrive on the lunch table looking perfect, and truly freshly baked.

I talk with Nicolas Berger in the comparative quiet after lunch service has finished. His admiration for Alain Ducasse is honest and quiet. "I know that it's pretty rare what we have here," he says. "It's because of Mr Ducasse that we're able to keep the quality of the bread."

Nicolas' father was a pastry chef, with a shop in a little village. Nicolas continued his father's traditions, but after a while he became fascinated by bread, too. "Fifteen years ago it was pejorative to say, 'I'm a pastry chef who also bakes bread', because the result was not that impressive then," he says. "But I don't agree with that at all today. Bread is so important for the whole meal, and it should be remarkable".

Oatcakes

The grey-green coloured oatcake, with its edges scorched ever so slightly in the oven, always has a place at my table. There is something about the dry, tender crumb that requires cheese or butter. Though we think of the oatcake as resolutely Scottish, when it is on a plate with Cheddar, Roquefort or Wensleydale, it becomes a bread with a universal, elemental flavour that does not distract from or taint the food served with it.

TIP Ideally, roll the dough out immediately, but if you can't you will find that the dough hardens. This isn't a problem; simply add a little more water to the dough and work this through with your fingertips until it is evenly combined, then roll it out.

250g fine oatmeal (100%)

¾ tsp fine sea salt (1.5%)

½ tsp bicarbonate of soda (0.5%)

20g unsalted butter or lard (8%)

100g water at 20°C (40%)

additional oatmeal for rolling

In a bowl, combine the oatmeal with the salt and bicarbonate of soda. Rub the butter or lard through the dry ingredients until all of the lumps have disappeared. Add the water and mix until you have a soft dough.

Sprinkle a little fine oatmeal on the work-surface and place the dough on top of it. Sprinkle more oatmeal over the dough. Using the heel of your hand, bash the dough out to flatten it, then sprinkle more oatmeal on the top and underneath. Using a rolling pin, roll the dough to 3–4mm thick. While doing this, constantly run a spatula underneath to make sure the dough isn't sticking to the work-surface. Cut out discs using a 7cm or 8cm cutter and put them on to a baking tray.

Preheat the oven to 200°C/400°F/gas mark 6. Bake in the centre of the oven for 30–40 minutes, or until the biscuits are tinged with brown around the circumference. Leave to cool on a wire rack.

Barley flatbread

FOR THE OVERNIGHT BATTER:
200g boiling water (400%)
50g barley flour (100%)

FOR THE DOUGH:
the batter (166%)
150g barley flour (100%)
1 tsp ground barley malt (see malted grains on page 38–39) (3%)
½ tsp fresh yeast, crumbled (2%)
½ tsp fine sea salt (2%)
additional barley flour for dusting

FOR THE OVERNIGHT BATTER Cool the water to 80°C, then, in a bowl, beat the barley flour into the water. Leave the mixture overnight, covered.

FOR THE DOUGH In a bowl, stir all the ingredients together until you have a soft dough. Scrape any remaining dough from your fingers into the bowl, cover, and leave in a warm place for 2 hours, or until the mixture has puffed up.

Lightly flour the work-surface and roll out the dough until it is about 5mm thick. Cut the dough into rectangles and place them on a baking tray, with a gap of 1cm between each one. Cover with a cloth and leave in a warm place for 45 minutes.

Preheat the oven to 210°C/410°F/gas mark 6½. Bake the biscuits for 15 minutes, then reduce the heat to 180°C/350°F/gas mark 4 and bake for a further 25 minutes, or until the barley breads are crisp and light. Cool an a wire rack and store in an airtight container.

These thin, brutal flat breads, with their strange, sweet barley-malt taste, would once have been a staple of a simple breakfast or supper, toasted and served hot and buttered alongside a cold bowl of buttermilk. The dough can be enriched with a little butter or lard to make a "fatty bread". In our affluent times, austere recipes serve as a reminder of simpler ways.

Salty and sour berry crispbread

200g wholewheat or spelt flour (66%)

100g soft white flour (34%)

¼ tsp bicarbonate of soda (0.5%)

¼ tsp baking powder (0.5%)

¼ tsp fine sea salt (0.5%)

30g unsalted butter, softened (10%)

80g dried sweetened berries, chopped (27%)

125g water at 20°C (42%)

1 tsp powdered dried cloudberries, or ground sumac or lemon zest

salt flakes for sprinkling

In a bowl, combine the two flours with the bicarbonate of soda, baking powder, and salt. Rub the softened butter into these dry ingredients until it is evenly incorporated and the mixture slightly resembles very fine breadcrumbs. Stir in the chopped berries, then add the water. Scrunch the dough together with your fingers so that it is evenly mixed.

Preheat the oven to 220°C/425°F/gas mark 7. Lightly dust the work-surface with flour. Cut the dough in half, and keep one half in the bowl covered with a cloth while you roll out the other. While you roll, keep checking that the dough isn't sticking to the work-surface, but use only a little flour to achieve this. Roll out the dough until it is about 5mm thick, then prick the surface all over with a fork. Use a sharp knife or pastry wheel to cut squares in the dough, roughly 10cm across. Brush the surface with a little water, then sprinkle on the powdered cloudberries (or sumac or lemon zest).

Transfer these squares to a tray lined with non-stick baking parchment, then sprinkle a few flakes of sea salt on the top of each. Bake for 10–12 minutes, until the breads are slightly puffed and tinged dark brown at the edges. While the breads are baking, roll out and finish the remaining dough.

Transfer the breads to a wire rack to cool. Store in an airtight container.

Johan Sörbergs, a remarkable young Swedish baker in Stockholm, makes very thin rye crispbreads dusted ever so lightly with a ground powder made from the local yellow cloudberry, which has an acid-fruity sharpness and a sulphurous colour that stains the top of the bread. I've combined this idea with putting berries in the bread, so doubling the flavour. Since it is hard to find cloudberries outside Scandinavia, other dried sharp berries can be used. Redcurrants, gooseberries or cranberries, though usually sweetened with sugar before drying, are suitable. Yet this sweetness loses the fruit's zing. A better replacement is the ground sumac spice found in Lebanese food shops. As a last resort, use grated lemon zest.

Scotland

Breadmaking is unlikely to involve invention, but it must depend on rediscovery. As part of this, bringing back old grains helps millers and farmers to practice traditional production methods by placing them in context. Traditional mills grind hard grains into flour in much the same way as they have for hundreds of years. The millstones that were used by our grandparents look much like the millstones that we use now in restored water or windmills. The grain may even make flour that tastes the same as it did then, though we will never really know that for sure.

Bere is a type of barley that was once widely cultivated for food in Scotland, Ireland, and parts of northern Europe. Though bere may have existed in Scotland since Neolithic times, it was probably introduced as a crop by the Vikings between 787 and 950. The name could have derived from the old Icelandic "barr", a type of local barley that was once cultivated there.

Bere is the root of other words in our language. The word "barn" means "barley place", and stems from a combination of barley (bere) and house (aern). The word beer was spelt "bere" during the Jacobean period, and previously by the Anglo-Saxons as "beor"; in Britain, beer is brewed by steeping sprouted and toasted barley grains in warm water that has been mixed with an infusion of hops, and then fermenting this concoction with yeast.

Together with oats, bere once formed an important part of the diet of Highland people, as both of these grains would grow in difficult Highland soils and ripen during a short growing season. Much like rye, bere did not bind into an elastic loaf that is capable of trapping air to make it light and crisp. Instead, it would be mixed into a batter, or patted out flat between the hands, and tossed on to a hot "girdle" to make a thin round loaf called a bannock. Oatcakes are made in a similar way, using oats.

It was difficult to keep the grain dry, though communities would dry it in a local "corn" kiln (corn was a term applied to all grain). With dampness, some grain would inevitably sprout, resulting in an unintentional malting, and sweetening, of the final flour. At home, bere would be scorched in a kettle over the fire to make it hard enough to grind.

Golspie Mill, a one-and-a-quarter-hour drive north of Inverness, is one place where bere and peasemeal (a flour made from yellow peas) are still kilned and milled traditionally. Michael Shaw spends a hectic few hours

ABOVE, CLOCKWISE FROM TOP: The release plug that allows the water to run down the mill laide; the hole where the grain enters the millstone; Munlochy Bay, opposite Donnie MacLeod's farm; the mill wall covered in vine tendrils. OPPOSITE, CLOCKWISE FROM TOP LEFT: across the mill pond at Golspie Mill; miller Michael Shaw standing in the kiln used to toast the bere meal; sacks of rye grain on the upper floor of the mill; the geese and the mill wheel; the wooden framework around the millstone; a wheatmeal, bere and oat loaf, stacked by the trout pond; Donnie MacLeod's dog, Bess. CENTRE: Michael and Becky Shaw.

LEFT TO RIGHT: a Prunus in blossom; farmer and activist Donnie MacLeod, of MacLeod Organics in Ardersier, on the Black Isle.

each morning running up and down the wooden stairs in a setting that resembles a bleached-wood Meccano set, making sure that the cogs turn, the sacks are lifted, and the stones rotate. His working hours are compressed because the source of power to turn the wheel – the water – is limited.

A small burn fills a mill pond approximately 30 metres across. This takes about a day to fill, though less time in the rainy seasons, when excess water overflows through the trout pond. To work the mill, a large plug on a chain is opened and the water runs down a narrow mill laide (race) to turn the wheel. A full mill pond gives about two hours of power, and during that time it is necessary to make the most of the energy that is provided by the turning wheel. Other than grinding the grains, the water powers various sieves, a fanner to blow the dust and husk off the grain, and a rope hoist to move the sacks of grain and flour between the floors.

I sat with Michael and his partner Becky around the old Aga in the miller's house. "I arrived from New Zealand and worked the first season as a shearer", said Michael. "Milling isn't something that, as a child, you'd think you would grow up and want to do, is it? It never even occurred to me that there would be such a thing happening."

The previous miller, Fergus, and his wife were retiring and they needed someone to take over. "Fergus showed me the mill and I thought: 'Wow, check this out!'", says Michael. "It had that grainy sort of smell. The bere was moving through my hands, cogs were turning, and belts were moving, and I thought: 'Oh yeah, this might be something to have a look at'. Other people were interested but we got selected over the, er, rivals."

Becky adds, laughing: "Fergus said that the others were from somewhere in England, and all they wanted to talk about was 'the money', and he straight away didn't like them."

Every so often, Michael takes a delivery of his flours to MacLeod Organics in Ardersier, the home and base of the farmer and activist Donnie MacLeod. The village sits on the shore of the Moray Firth, and is so close to the sea that you can feel the salt drying your skin, and the sea air cleansing your eyes and breath. Early in 2002, Donnie was arrested for failing to co-operate after refusing to move from a GM crop trial, and the subsequent press support turned him into a local hero. For now, the trial is on hold.

We take a ride out on his tractor around the paddocks, as he feeds his cows organic carrots dug from his fields. "The cows really love carrots", he says, as they rush around the back of the trailer that tips piles of orange roots on to the green grass and clover.

MacLeod Organics delivers boxes of organic vegetables and ingredients to customers in the area, and among the onions, potatoes, and seasonal vegetables, Golspie Mill's packets of oatmeal, wholemeal flour, beremeal, and peasemeal can also be ordered. One of Donnie's customers is a local family on a low income who bake at home; in return for an organic box they help around the farm with bits of weeding.

"When people talk about our national health insurance, that 'insurance' is in our soil", says Donnie. "The seeds, grains, plants, and the wildlife that depends on them must be kept protected from chemical harm. It is that pure food our children must be allowed to eat, and I will fight for that to be."

Anchovy buttons

These small biscuits, each with a nugget of butter-cooked anchovy nestling in the centre, are good to serve with a glass of cold beer. Beef dripping makes the taste of breads like this more full and rich than their ingredients might suggest.

TIP This recipe is open to variations according to what you have or like to eat. You could use butter or good pork lard instead of beef dripping. If millet is difficult to find, then cornmeal or ground rice could be substituted.

250g soft white flour (83%)

50g finely ground millet (17%)

½ tsp bicarbonate of soda (1%)

½ tsp fine sea salt (1%)

75g beef dripping (25%)

90g water at 20°C (30%)

FOR THE ANCHOVY BUTTER:

15g unsalted butter

3–4 good anchovies, finely chopped

a sliver of garlic

In a bowl, combine the flour, millet, soda, and salt. Using your fingers, work the dripping into the dry ingredients until the mixture resembles coarse breadcrumbs. Slowly add the water, and work it in until you have a soft, smooth dough.

Lightly flour the work-surface and roll the dough to 3–4mm thick. Using a 4cm round cutter, cut disks from the dough and lift them with a knife on to a parchment-lined tray.

Preheat the oven to 200°C/400°F/gas mark 6. Place the anchovies, butter and garlic in a small saucepan and heat until the butter melts and the mixture begins to sizzle. Remove from the heat and allow to cool a little, then, using a pastry brush or a teaspoon, spread a little anchovy butter over the surface of each biscuit. The idea is to lightly coat the surface so it flavours the biscuit without running down the sides. Finally, dot a small piece of anchovy in the centre of each biscuit.

Bake in the centre of the oven for 20 minutes, or until the biscuits have just started to colour. Remove from the tray and cool on a wire rack. When cold, store in an airtight container.

Rosemary and fresh cheese sticks

Salty food, served late in the afternoon, brings on a thirst and provides an excuse to drink a cocktail or *apéritif*. These slivers of dough, made from a mixture flavoured and moistened with soft fresh cheese and the oily herb rosemary, are generously salted. In Italy, there are many versions of what they call *grissini*, sometimes plain, sometimes light and open-textured. At Giorgio Locatelli's restaurant in London, *grissini* are tipped with a shaving of the best ham from Parma, making them perfect to sit in a flute on a table, to be served with a glass of dry Prosecco or sparkling water.

TIP Other herbs can be used to flavour this bread. Try adding the following to the dough: lemon thyme, marjoram, sage or chives, cut fine.

FOR THE FERMENT:

150g soft white flour (100%)

250g whole milk (166%)

¾ tsp fresh yeast, crumbled (3%)

FOR THE DOUGH:

250g soft flour (100%)

1 tsp fine sea salt (2%)

80g unsalted butter (32%)

50g fresh curd cheese, such as ricotta (20%)

large sprig of rosemary, chopped (2%)

the ferment (162%)

FOR THE FERMENT In a bowl, combine all the ingredients and leave in a warm place for 1 hour.

FOR THE DOUGH In a bowl, combine the flour with the salt. Rub the butter, cheese, and rosemary into the dry ingredients until the butter and cheese are evenly mixed. This rubbing will help the rosemary release its aromatic oil into the flour.

Stir the ferment into the flour mixture, and scrunch the dough together with your hands until evenly mixed. Scrape any remaining dough from your fingers into the bowl, cover and leave for 10 minutes.

Rub 1 tsp of corn or olive oil on the work-surface and knead the dough on the oiled surface for 10 seconds, ending with a smooth, round ball. Wipe the bowl clean, replace the dough, cover and leave for a further 10 minutes. Repeat this light kneading twice more at 10-minute intervals. Then leave the dough for 1 hour, kneading it once more during that time.

Preheat the oven to 180°C/350°F/gas mark 4. Lightly flour the work-surface and roll the dough out into a 20 x 30cm rectangle. Cut thin strips across the width of the dough, each less than a centimetre thick, then roll these with your hands on the work-surface so they elongate and become strands of dough about 40cm long. Lay them on a tray lined with non-stick baking parchment, leaving a little space in-between so they do not stick together when they expand in the oven.

Bake in the centre of the oven for 25–30 minutes, or until the sticks are crisp and golden brown. With my oven, it helps to flip the sticks over three-quarters of the way through the cooking so that they get evenly coloured. Remove the sticks from the tray and leave to cool on a wire rack while you bake the remainder.

White bean wafer

This thin crispbread uses that old standby for the humble loaf, the bean. When there was insufficient flour to make a loaf, or where the local flour was coarse and unappetizing, the addition of either cooked beans or rice added bulk to the dough and softened the taste. Now we know it would have also increased the nutritional content of the bread, making it higher in protein and good for a diet with little meat or fish. Serve with a fresh tomato salad, good when the new season's tomatoes are ripe and peppery from the vine, and a few soft olives.

TIP Try other cooked pulses, such as chickpeas or borlotti beans, and combine them with herbs or paprika.

200g cooked white beans, drained well and dried on kitchen towel (100%)
200g soft white flour (100%)
½ tsp bicarbonate of soda (1%)
½ tsp baking powder (1%)
¾ tsp fine sea salt (1.5%)
50g unsalted butter (25%)
30g water at 20°C (15%)
sea salt flakes

Using a mortar and pestle, or a food processor, mash the beans until you have a fine, smooth paste. In a bowl, combine the flour, soda, baking powder, and salt. Rub the butter into these dry ingredients, then add the bean paste and water, working them in well with your fingers until you have a soft, smooth dough.

Preheat the oven to 200°C/400°F/gas mark 6. Roll out the dough on a floured work-surface until it is 3–4mm thick. Cut the dough into rectangles measuring 5 x 10cm, and place these on a baking tray lined with non-stick parchment. Brush a little water down the centre of each wafer, and sprinkle a line of sea salt flakes down the middle of each.

Bake in the centre of the oven for 15–20 minutes, or until the biscuits are lightly brown at the edges. Transfer to a wire rack and leave in a warm place so that they continue to dry and become crisp. When cold, store in an airtight container.

The finish

Often, prior to baking, I leave a loaf crusted in the flour that protected the dough from the cloth. But an extra dusting of coarse semolina or wholewheat flour, or a light brush with olive oil, can elevate the crust. These recipes will help you perfect that special finish.

Custard for baking

400g fresh milk
1 vanilla pod, split and seeds scraped out
25g cornflour
125g caster sugar
2 medium eggs
50g unsalted butter, softened

In a saucepan, heat the milk with the vanilla pod and its seeds and scrapings until hot and nearly boiling. Remove from the heat and leave to infuse for 5 minutes. Remove the pod.

In a bowl, mix the cornflour with the sugar. Beat in the eggs, one at a time, until smooth and combined. Whisk the hot milk into the mixture, return to the saucepan, and heat, whisking constantly, until it comes to the boil. Remove from the heat, transfer immediately into a cooler container, and beat in the softened butter.

Press a piece of buttered paper (or the butter wrapper) on to the surface of the custard and then leave to cool.

Starch glaze

The brilliantine of loaf finishes, this starch glaze gives a polished appearance to the loaf and was much used at the beginning of the 20th century. Simply a boiled mixture of starch and water, it sets quickly in the oven and creates a smooth varnish that gives the loaf a satin sheen after baking.

50g cornflour or potato starch
200g water

Mix the cornflour with a few tablespoons of the water to soften it, then whisk in the remaining water. Place this mixture in a saucepan and bring to the boil, stirring constantly. Remove from the heat and leave to cool.

To use, brush the loaf with the glaze about 15 minutes before the end of baking.

Egg glaze

It was in the Ukraine where I first saw a baker tie together a few long chicken feathers to make a simple brush. The brush was then dipped into a cup which contained a fresh egg whisked into a vivid orange wash for the top of the loaf (see above). The chickens fed on the crusts of bread, beetles, and corncobs, and the enrichment of both the crust and crumb of the loaf by the eggs, gave a strong sense of their place in that family's nourishment.

Bakers have different preferences when brushing the unbaked loaf with egg. Some prefer just the yolks, mixed with the same weight of cold water and a pinch of salt. This gives a very strongly coloured wash that darkens quickly in the oven and retains the mark of the brush when baked. Others use the whole egg, beaten – sometimes with a little milk – which will give a gentle, golden sheen to the baked loaf. Usually the flavour of the egg remains, so make sure it's fresh, and don't leave the wash sitting around for too long before using it, as it can soon develop an "off" aroma.

Salt-water wash

This will give a salty crust to small rolls or a large loaf and is best used in combination with a reduction in the amount of salt in the dough.

100g boiling water
50g fine sea salt

Pour the boiling water over the salt, and stir until the salt has dissolved. Apply with a pastry brush just before baking.

Boiled sugar glaze

The sticky sweet glaze of a boiled syrup is often part of the appeal of sweet buttery breads. It is drenched on after baking but, once the bread is cold, it stays glossy and sticks to everything the loaf touches. If you brush it on while the loaf is still hot, it tends to crystallize and dry white and matt.

150g caster sugar
100g water

Warm the sugar and water together in a saucepan, stirring until the sugar has dissolved. Bring the syrup to the boil and simmer for 2 minutes. Remove from the heat and leave undisturbed to cool.

Dusting with icing or caster sugar

Some breads can be dusted with icing or caster sugar just before baking, particularly those enriched breads that are baked for a short time. Don't think this is simply for sweet breads, however; the salty biscuit dusted in sugar is an odd but good chew. Place either sugar in a tea-strainer or sieve, on a plate. Then carefully lift the sieve over the bread and gently dredge the sugar over the top of the loaf, roll or biscuit.

Coarse-grain or seed crust

Flaked wheat, rolled oats or seeds are good on the outside of a loaf. The way to stick them on is to roll the unbaked loaf on a wet cloth lying on a tray, then in one swift move roll the loaf again on a tray covered with your chosen grain or seed. This light coating of water makes the grain or seed stick, and gives a very smart cloak to the crust of the loaf.

Alcohol wash

Sometimes dough is brushed with alcohol before baking to stick sugar, say, to the crust so that only its underlying flavour remains and the spirit evaporates in the oven. Other times it is brushed or poured on to the loaf after baking. At Maison Bertaux, an old Anglo-French pastry shop in London's Soho district, they keep a bottle of rum by the cash till for dousing each baba as it is sold. Lovely.

Butter-crumb crust

Breadcrumbs can be used as a crust on a loaf in the same way as grains and seeds. Flavourings, such as garlic, anchovy, ground black pepper or paprika can be added to the crumbs.

250g coarse or fine breadcrumbs
50g melted butter
½ tsp fine sea salt

Place the breadcrumbs in a bowl and pour the melted butter over them. Stir, add the salt, then rub the crumbs in your hands to make sure the butter and salt are evenly combined. Spread these out on a tray and then, as with the grain method, roll the unbaked loaf on a wet cloth before rolling it in the buttered crumbs.

WEIGHT		VOLUME		
metric	**imperial**	**metric**	**imperial**	
5g	⅛oz	1.25ml	¼ teaspoon	
10g	¼oz	2.5ml	½ teaspoon	
15g	½oz	5ml	1 teaspoon	
25-30g	1oz	10ml	2 teaspoon	
35g	1¼oz	15ml	½ fl oz	
40g	1½oz	30ml	1fl oz	
50g	1¾oz	50ml	2fl oz	
55g	2oz	75ml	2½ fl oz	
60g	2¼oz	100ml	3½ fl oz	
70g	2½oz	125ml	4 fl oz	
85g	3oz	150ml	5 fl oz	¼ pint
90g	3¼oz	175ml	6 fl oz	
100g	3½oz	200 ml	7 fl oz	⅓ pint
115g	4oz	225 ml	8fl oz	
125g	4½oz	250ml	9 fl oz	
140g	5oz	300ml	10fl oz	½ pint
150g	5½oz	350ml	12fl oz	
175g	6oz	400ml	14fl oz	
200g	7oz	425ml	15fl oz	¾ pint
225g	8oz	450ml	16fl oz	
250g	9oz	500ml	18fl oz	
275g	9¾oz	600ml	20fl oz	1 pint
280g	10oz	700ml	1¼ pints	
300g	10½oz	850ml	1½ pints	
325g	11½oz	1 litre	1¾ pints	
350g	12oz	1.2 litres	2 pints	
375g	13oz	1.3 litres	2¼ pints	
400g	14oz	1.4 litres	2½ pints	
425g	15oz	1.5 litres	2¾ pints	
450g	1lb	1.7 litres	3 pints	
500g	1lb 2oz			
550g	1lb 4oz			
600g	1lb 5oz			
650g	1lb 7oz			
700g	1lb 9oz			
750g	1lb 10oz			
800g	1lb 12oz			
850g	1lb 14oz			
900g	2lb			
950g	2lb 2oz			
1kg	2lb 4oz			
1.25kg	2lb 12oz			
1.3kg	3lb			
1.5kg	3lb 5oz			
1.6kg	3lb 8oz			
1.8kg	4lb			
2kg	4lb 8oz			
2.25kg	5lb			
2.5kg	5lb 8oz			
2.7kg	6lb			
3kg	6lb 8oz			

These charts are reproduced with the kind permission of The Guild of Food Writers.

Author's acknowledgments

To my editor Rebecca Spry, for her patience, and to Yasia Williams, Lawrence Morton and Hattie Ellis, thanks for working so hard and taking the effort to make it good; my friends Dean Brettschneider, Richard Whittington, and Richard Bertinet for their encouragement and humour through it all; Giorgio and Plaxi Locatelli, Federico Turi, Federico Sali, and the staff at Locanda Locatelli; Susan Low and Guy Dimond; Wendy Fogarty; Patricia and Paul Harrison at Ceci Paolo, Ledbury, www.cecipaolo.com; Marie and Nick Daffern and their family at Hope End, www.hopeend.com; Troels Bendix, www.breadsetcetera.com; Sylvia MacDonald and Gary Parker at the British Baker; Chris Smail, Karen Tilley, Neville Moon, Rachel Saunders, and the staff at Bakehouse; Judy and David Horgan, Adrian Watson, Murray Rhind, and the bakers at Café Royal, Newcastle; Sharron, Tamara, and Evelyn at Snappy Snaps, Tooting; Colin Bradbury and the staff at Genie Imaging, www.genieimaging.co.uk; Clive Mellum and John Lister at Shipton Mill; and Alastair Hendy for putting me in a good light.

FOR HELP WITH THE SCIENCE: Ian Roberts, Chris Bond, and the staff at the National Collection of Yeast Cultures, Norwich, www.ncyc.co.uk; Professor Peter Shewry from Rothamsted Research, Harpenden, www.rothamsted.bbsrc.ac.uk; Dr. James Barnett; Keith Wooller at ADM Milling.

TO THE FOLLOWING BAKERS, MILLERS, FARMERS, AND FAMILIES:
SWEDEN: Dag Hermelin, Lisa Förare Winbladh, Johan Sörbergs at Riddarbageriet, Stockholm; Robert Saberski at Roslagsbröd, Gimo, www.roslagsbrod.se; Jan Hedh, Olof Viktors, Glemmingebro, www.olofviktors.se; Östen Brolin, Vete-Katten, Stockholm, www.vetekatten.se;
DENMARK: Camilla Plum and Per Koelster, Fuglebjerggaard, Helsinge, www.fuglebjerggaard.dk;
FRANCE: Nicolas Berger and his staff, Hélène Barbier and Emmanuelle Perrier, for Alain Ducasse, Hôtel Plaza Athénée, www.plaza-athenee-paris.com;
IRELAND: Michael Power and Ann Sutton, The Bakehouse, New Ross, Co. Wexford; Will Sutherland and Angela Ashe, School for Self Sufficiency; Killowen, New Ross, Co. Wexford, www.self-sufficiency.net;
SCOTLAND: Mike and Becky Shaw, Golspie Mill, Sutherland, www.golspiemill.co.uk; Donnie MacLeod, MacLeod Organics, Ardersier, Inverness, www.macleodorganics.com;
GERMANY: Isa Petereit, Julia Decker; Franz Stricker, Klenstrasse 69, Munich;
RUSSIA: Lilia Smelkolva at Slow Food, Bra, Italy; Ekaterina Drozdova; William Webster; Sofia Shurovskaia; Jonathan Thatcher;
UKRAINE: Paul Okopsky and Ukrainian Travel, www.Ukraine.co.uk; Mrs Yaroslava Kharuk and her son Andre, and the staff at Manchester Café, Ivano-Frankivsk; Oxana Yefimchuk; Igor Aveolyan; Mother Theresa and the Congregation of Sisters Meronocyts, Ivano-Frankivsk;
ITALY: Toni Vitiello, Claudio, Stella at Focacceria Tipica Ligure, Torino; Silvia Capello; Marta Bera at Panetteria Bera; the staff at Latteria Bera Bruna;
ENGLAND: Jack and Jill Lang; Andy Lynes at www.egullet.com; Jim Webb, Yotam, Noam, and the staff at Ottolenghi; Michael Stoate, Cann Mills, Dorset; Aiden Chapman and the staff at Leakers bakery; Emmanuel Hadjiandreou at Daylesford Farm, Gloucestershire.

Flour and grain stockists

SHIPTON MILL and their mail order service Flour Direct, that will ship in the UK and around the world the selection of flours used in this book, as well as malt, chopped rye, and malted cut rye. Long Newnton, Tetbury, Gloucestershire, GL8 8RP, 01666 505050 enquiries@shipton-mill.com.

MALT: Dried ground malt powder is available at Muntons, the maltsters in Stowmarket, who sell through home brewing suppliers around the UK. Their Spraymalt range is good for baking, and can be used wherever ground dried malt is called for in a recipe. For stockists telephone 01449 618 362.

FRESH YEAST: Most supermarkets and bakeries where dough-mixing and baking is done on site, sell fresh yeast. In the case of small shop bakers, do respect their need to sell their bread. Ask to buy a loaf, and a little fresh yeast as well.